101 Ways to Find Work...And Keep Finding Work for the Rest of Your Career!

Dr. Charles Michael Austin

Cengage Learning PTR

CENGAGE
Learning·

Professional • Technical • Reference

Australia, Brazil, Japan, Korea, Mexico, Singapore, Spain, United Kingdom, United States

CENGAGE Learning®

Professional • Technical • Reference

**101 Ways to Find Work...
And Keep Finding
Work for the Rest
of Your Career!**
**Dr. Charles Michael
Austin**

**Publisher and
General Manager,
Cengage Learning PTR:**
Stacy L. Hiquet

**Associate Director
of Marketing:**
Sarah Panella

**Manager of
Editorial Services:**
Heather Talbot

**Senior Marketing
Manager:**
Mark Hughes

Senior Product Manager:
Mitzi Koontz

Project and Copy Editor:
Kate Shoup

Interior Layout:
Shawn Morningstar

Cover Designer:
Luke Fletcher

Proofreader:
Sam Garvey

Printed in the United
States of America
1 2 3 4 5 6 7 16 15 14

For product information and technology
assistance, contact us at
**Cengage Learning Customer and Sales Support,
1-800-354-9706.**

For permission to use material from this
text or product, submit all requests online at
cengage.com/permissions.

Further permissions questions can be
e-mailed to **permissionrequest@cengage.com.**

All trademarks are the property of their respective
owners.

All images © Cengage Learning unless otherwise noted.

Library of Congress Control Number: 2014932074
ISBN-13: 978-1-305-11136-3
ISBN-10: 1-305-11136-2

Cengage Learning PTR
20 Channel Center Street
Boston, MA 02210
USA

Cengage Learning is a leading provider of customized learning solutions with office locations around the globe, including Singapore, the United Kingdom, Australia, Mexico, Brazil, and Japan. Locate your local office at: **international.cengage.com/region.**

Cengage Learning products are represented in Canada by Nelson Education, Ltd.

For your lifelong learning solutions, visit **cengageptr.com.**
Visit our corporate Web site at **cengage.com.**

For Werner, Sigmund, and Timothy
for their inspiration.

For Richard Clarke, my "older brother"
who died too soon.

And always for Monica, the
"look-forward-to" every day of my life.

Acknowledgments

Any book is a collaboration…. Thank you to Stu Miller, the best literary agent ever. Thank you to Mitzi Koontz of Cengage Learning for her courage and support. Thank you to Kate Shoup. A first-rate editor is a gift, and Kate has been wonderful. Thank you to my colleagues and friends Tom Lenzo, Bobby Borg, Ronny Schiff, and Dan Kimpel. You are all a joy to know and to work with.

About the Author

Dr. Charles Michael Austin (or "Dr. Chaz," as he is known) counsels private clients and serves as a mentor and college professor specializing in career development. He has taught business and communication courses at institutions of higher learning in southern California since 1998, including the Fashion Institute of Design & Merchandising, Phillips Graduate Institute, The Art Institute–Hollywood and Los Angeles, Glendale Community College, Chapman University, and Loyola Marymount University.

Dr. Austin served as Career Resource Specialist for business students and alumni at Woodbury University in Burbank, MBA Career Development and Employer Relations Manager at Pepperdine University's School of Business and Management, and Director of Placement at Video Symphony in Burbank. He currently serves as Director of Career Development at Musicians Institute in Hollywood, CA, where he supervises the career development staff as well as creating, developing, and teaching career development courses. He has presented papers on the subject of career development to the National Association of Women MBAs, the Association for Business Communication, the National Council for Workforce Education, the Society of Educators and Scholars, and the International College Teaching and Learning Conference.

Dr. Austin holds a B.A. in Sociology from The City College of New York, an M.A. in Broadcast Communication Arts from San Francisco State University, and a doctorate in Organizational Leadership from Pepperdine University.

Contents

Part 4

Part 5

Part 6

Contents

Part 7

Networking **76**

Part 8

Time Management **91**

Part 9

Organization (Yours and Theirs) **95**

Part 10

Part 11

Part 12

Part 13

Contents

Part 14

Part 15

Part 16

Introduction

The days of corporate loyalty are over. The working world has become a freelance world. Whatever field you're in, you will always have to hustle for work. You yourself are a business. And like any business, you are a brand. That means you must be trained to define, articulate, and sell that brand. This book is your guide.

In this book, I'll provide practical, relevant, and valuable mentoring. I'm not only a leading authority in the field of career development, but I hire and manage people. This book contains advice you can use at any stage in your life, whatever you do, for as long as you choose to work.

This book explores the following:

- How to move your job search into the 21st century

- Distinguishing needs from wants

- Managing time and money

- Why you don't need to worry if you don't know what you want to do

- Getting inside the boss's head so she'll hire you

- Building a granular database, the foundation of all your networking

- How to stay sane while you search for work

Who This Book Is For

I've taught and counseled all manner of professionals of all ages, from graphic artists to fashion designers to chefs to musicians to financial consultants to filmmakers. In doing so, I've learned that the same principles apply to every industry and occupation. Whatever you do, whether you're an intern or a business owner, or dream of doing, you're going to need to sell your services. *101 Ways to Find Work…and Keep Finding Work for the Rest of Your Career!* will teach you how.

How This Book Is Organized

This book is organized into 16 chapters:

- Chapter 1, "The Context." This chapter gets you grounded in the new world of work.

- Chapter 2, "Moving Your Job-Seeking Strategy into the 21st Century." Here, you'll explore the wide world of freelancing—and how you can make it your own.

- Chapter 3, "The Importance of Passion." This chapter is all about passion—how to find it, how to feed it, and why it's okay if you haven't hit on yours just yet.

- Chapter 4, "The Employer's Perspective." This chapter unlocks the mysteries of the interview.

- Chapter 5, "Communication." As you'll learn in this chapter, communication is the key to your success.

- Chapter 6, "Résumés and Cover Letters." Here, you'll learn how to write and use your résumé and cover letters—even though they don't matter so much anymore.

- Chapter 7, "Networking." Networking helps you connect with others, not just for your own benefit, but for theirs, too.

- Chapter 8, "Time Management." This chapter is about focus and the myth of procrastination.

- Chapter 9, "Organization (Yours and Theirs)." Read this chapter for tips about navigating the working world. (Hint: It's all politics.)

- Chapter 10, "Getting Out of Your Own Way." Read this chapter to learn how your friends can keep you from shooting yourself in the foot.

- Chapter 11, "Building a Name for Yourself in Your Field." For tips on making a name for yourself, read this chapter.

- Chapter 12, "Continuing to Learn and Improve." No matter how old you are, you must never stop learning. Read this chapter for tips on staying on top of your career and your life.

- Chapter 13, "Staying Sane." Looking for work is tough, but it's never that bad. This chapter features tips to help you stay sane during your job search.

- Chapter 14, "Premium Marketing Strategies." Even if you have a "traditional" job, you're still your own business. This chapter features high-end coaching ideas to help market yourself.

- Chapter 15, "More Artillery." Sometimes you need to get creative and bring out the big guns. This chapter features tips that you may not have thought of before.

- Chapter 16, "Building Your Online Footprint." This chapter is all about embracing the future and making friends everywhere.

1

THE CONTEXT

The mediocre teacher tells. The good teacher explains. The superior teacher demonstrates. The great teacher inspires.
—William Arthur Ward, Author (1921–1994)

There is a sign in my office that says, "Welcome to the Tough Love Dispensary." Well, reader, welcome to my office—in book form. *101 Ways to Find Work* is straight talk on how to deal with the working world the way it really is, not how we'd like it to be. As a career mentor and educator who is dedicated to preparing my clients to be successful, to supporting and empowering them to make their dreams come true, I can do no less. There are things in this book that you may not *want* to hear, but I believe you *need* to hear (or, more accurately, read).

Whatever your vocational goals, whatever stage you are in your career—whether it's just beginning or you're close to retiring but you can't afford to stop making money—this book will help you get from here to there, turning your dreams and fantasies into actions and results.

I'm known among my colleagues as "the human alarm clock" because I wake people up to what's possible in themselves and in the world. I hold three degrees: a B.A. in Sociology, an M.A. in Broadcast Communication Arts (Radio and Television), and an Ed.D. in Organizational Leadership. I've worked with literally hundreds of clients and students—from teenagers to adults in their sixties—at 16 (and counting) different colleges and universities. I know that, with the exception of retirees who "always wanted to take a film course" at their local community college, all students go to school for primarily one reason: to increase their earning power.

Everything I teach—and everything in this book—is designed to impart practical, relevant knowledge and practices that you can use forever to help you make more money doing satisfying, fulfilling work that you love (or at least enjoy).

NOTE *I deliberately use the word "knowledge" rather than "informa-tion." We have a lot of information about the activities of celebrities but, while gossip is fun, this information doesn't improve our lives. Knowledge, on the other hand, is something we can use to better ourselves. As Yale librarian Rutherford D. Rogers put it, "We're drowning in information and starving for knowledge."*

Let's get to it....

1.
Distinguish What Is from the Way You'd Like Things to Be

Way back in the 20th century, people worked for one company, moved up through the ranks, and after about 30 years, they retired and received a gold watch and a pension. Wouldn't it be nice if life was still like that? Unfortunately, few of us will ever be able to afford to retire, and those gold watches and pensions have become a relic of the past.

Welcome to the 21st century, where everyone is a freelancer, and we're all hustling for work, *all the time*. You don't want that to be true or like the fact that it is? Too bad. The universe doesn't care what you want. If you doubt me, drive into the desert one night. When you've left civilization behind and it's just you and the stars in the sky, get out of your car. Stand there and tell the universe what you want…and notice how profoundly indifferent the universe is to your request.

You need to get with the program whether you like it or not. Adapt or die. (Well, not literally *die*, but find your options shrinking.) As a college professor, I don't like the rise of massive open online courses (MOOCs). If they prove successful, the result will be fewer professors in the classroom—a threat to my livelihood. And you know what? No one cares what I think. MOOCs are the future. I can either figure out a way to get on the train (that is, participate in the future) or discover that there won't be work for me.

This is tip #1 because where you want to start on your quest for work (or any quest in your life, for that matter) is by recontextualizing. In vernacular terms, you need to know where you are before you know where you're going, or know the lay of the land, or have some perspective *before* you begin your journey. As the American writer Henry Miller (1891–1980) said, "The world is not to be put in order; the world is order, incarnate. It is for us to harmonize with this order."

As I tell my students (and I guess you're now one of them), if you want perfection, if you want it to all work out, go see a movie. And by the way, since you're at the beginning of your quest, know that you can do all the right things and still not get what you want. There are no guarantees. *You* have to decide that it's worth the battle. Some days, you'll lose the drive. You won't feel like it. You won't be motivated. You won't *want* to. And that's when you'll need to *recommit* to your goal.

It's sad but true: Life's a bitch and then you die. I believe there is no inherent meaning in anything. The only meaning is the meaning we give things—in other words, our interpretation. Well then, you say, what's the point of anything, if it's all meaningless? My answer to you is, imagine the freedom in knowing that you can create any interpretation you like of any person or interaction or circumstance. Hopefully, you'll create interpretations that empower you and the people around you. Either way, a perspective, a context, like this allows you to create and *re*create every day. Underlying all of this is the knowledge that you have a unique set of talents and skills that you are obliged to share with the world.

So it's not about you and how you feel about the way things are; it's about the quest. As I write this, I'm sitting on a beautiful deck in a beautiful house in sunny southern California, on vacation for a few days. I'm human, too; the last thing I want to do today is work. I told my dear wife, "I'm not motivated to write today." And her response was, "So write anyway." For me, just like for you, it's not about how I feel, it's about my quest to help you. My goal is to have my experience, thoughts, and words contribute to your life to empower you to make your dreams come true.

2.

Know the Difference Between Needs and Wants

I know, you need that latte from Starbucks every morning or you just can't get started with your day. No you don't. You *want* it. What you *need* to do is pay the rent and put gas in your car and buy groceries.

Picture your body. When you get cold, what gets cold first? Your extremities—your hands and feet. The human body is designed that way to protect the vital organs (your heart, lungs, etc.). In your life and career, your "vital organs" are your commitments—the goals you have. Everything you do needs to focus on accomplishing them. That means you will need to choose how you prioritize your time and money. That's not to say you can *never* have that latte. Maybe you'll need to cut back to once a week and invest the balance in a software upgrade that will help you attract more clients. Maybe you can't go out drinking with your friends twice a week because your time would be better spent resting and preparing for a client presentation in the morning. Whatever it is, you will need to make some sacrifices to accomplish your long-term goals.

3.

Learn by Doing

I have a philosophy behind all my teaching and coaching, and it's this: I don't think we learn much by memorizing facts, or reading theories, or taking tests, or doing busy work, or writing essays, or reading, or hearing about others' experiences, or any of the other things that have been hallmarks of formal education in this country for decades. Rather, I think we learn through experience.

In school, most of us were taught using rote learning (also called "cognitive learning" or "didactic learning"), the goal of which is to have the teacher transmit information to the student. "Open head, pour in information, close head," as my friend Dr. Elizabeth Trebow describes it. But think of anything you do well (riding a bike, baking a cake, etc.). Remember how well you did it the first time you tried it and compare that to how much better you do it now. How I think we really learn is by practicing and rehearsing, by doing—over and over and over. Experiential learning is about meaningful, immersive, and long-lasting learning. It's knowledge that's relevant, pervasive, and applied. It creates muscle memory, so it sticks with you.

Don't take my word for it:

> We are what we repeatedly do. Excellence, then, is not an act, but a habit.
>
> —Aristotle, Greek philosopher (384–322 B.C.E.)

> You practice and you get better. It's very simple.
>
> —Philip Glass, American composer (1937–)

Given that your work and career are something you want to do, the more you do it, the better you'll get. And although practicing isn't necessarily fun, it does get you where you want to go.

This is true for everything in life, including "perfecting" your craft—and selling it. And one of the things I've learned about learning is that you don't have to *enjoy* the process in order to improve. There is a trend in American education that says that a student needs to enjoy the process in order to learn. I don't agree. It doesn't have to be fun. I study swing dancing. For someone well educated, it's a humbling process. My teacher shows me the steps for a new move. I try it, and invariably I don't do it correctly. She shows me again. I try again and fail again. This goes on over and over again until I finally do get the move. And then it becomes—and remains—part of my dance routine. Is it worth the effort? Absolutely. My wife's favorite activity is dancing, so seeing the smile on her face when we do a new move on the dance floor makes it all worthwhile. It's not about me; it's about her.

When you're always driven to reach your goal, you are unstoppable. No amount of frustration will deter you for long. The journey becomes about the joy of discovering what is possible and accomplishing things you never thought you could do. Don't let others' labels (including your own) limit who you can be. You'll be amazed at what you can accomplish!

In The Karate Kid (1984), the main character, Daniel, is a high-school senior transplanted to the suburbs of Los Angeles, and Mr. Miyagi is the Okinawan handyman in Daniel's apartment building. Mr. Miyagi becomes Daniel's martial arts teacher. He begins Daniel's training by having him perform menial tasks, including waxing cars, sanding a wooden walkway, and painting a fence at Mr. Miyagi's house. Each chore is accompanied with specific breathing and body movements, including clockwise and counter-clockwise and up-and-down hand motions. Daniel fails to see any connection between his chores and martial arts; he believes Mr. Miyagi has just been using him as slave labor. When he complains, Mr. Miyagi shows Daniel that by doing these chores, Daniel has been learning defensive blocks through muscle memory. You may remember Mr. Miyagi's oft-repeated instruction to Daniel, "Wax on, wax off."

Having been a student for 20 years (with three degrees to show for it) and having taught more than 60 different courses (not just classes, but courses—everything from Criminology to The History of Rock 'N' Roll), it's been my experience that most of us learn not by memorizing information and being tested on our ability to regurgitate it, or by studying theories, but by doing.

MOVING YOUR JOB-SEEKING STRATEGY INTO THE 21ST CENTURY

We need to prepare our kids for a 21st century economy, and we're not doing it with our schools.

—Al Franken, United States Senator (1951–)

Way back in the 20th century, an education consisted of course after course after course, eventually leading to a diploma or degree. Sadly, not much has changed. Many people still wonder why they worked so hard and for so long, why they spent so much time and money, and what they received in return—besides debt. Similarly, back then, getting an interview was all about submitting a good résumé and a strong cover letter and then waiting to hear back. That worked back then, but it no longer applies. This chapter includes tips to help you move your education and job-seeking strategy into the 21st century.

9

4.

Identify the Importance and Meaning of Work

Sigmund Freud (1856–1939), the founder of psychoanalysis, said, "No other technique for the conduct of life attaches the individual so firmly to reality as laying emphasis on work, for his work at least gives him a secure place in a portion of reality, in the human community."

All of us have gifts we need to share with others. You want to do whatever it takes to be able to contribute your gifts to the world. Artists speak about their art coming through them—that they are not the source, but the vessel, and the source is some form of higher power.

As American dancer and choreographer Martha Graham (1894–1991) said, "There is a vitality, a life force, an energy, a quickening that is translated through you into action, and because there is only one of you in all time, this expression is unique. And if you block it, it will never exist through any other medium and will be lost...."

Doing productive work puts us into the flow of life. We help make things happen and move things forward. We are connected to and collaborating with others. Work gives our life purpose and meaning. And if it's work we enjoy doing, it gives us a reason to get up in the morning, because we know we are doing something others need. Whether that's teaching children how to add numbers, unloading freight on a dock, or serving coffee to busy travelers on their way to catch a plane, work tells us we've done some good for someone today.

So how do you identify your own gifts? You begin by noticing what it is you enjoy. What's fun for you? What kind of work would you do if money were not a factor? There may be more than one answer to these questions, and that's okay. Some people have multiple talents, and many—maybe most—of us will have more than one career in our lifetimes. Knowing this may bring some comfort if you're not sure what it is you want to do. I give you permission to *not* know.

Pick three fields or industries in which you are interested, are curious about, or think you might like to work in. Then start researching them. Read about them. Find the leading associations in the field. *Every* industry has trade associations. Do you enjoy eating potato chips? Have you ever wondered how they were made and thought you might want to become involved in that? If so, then you'll want to contact the United States Potato Board and the Snack Food Association (which publishes *Snack World* magazine). Most importantly, talk to people who work in—or who know someone who knows someone who works in—the field. Then meet with those people and learn from them what it's really like to work in that industry. Not the sanitized version depicted in movies and on television, but the "dirt."

As you explore each of these fields and begin meeting people who work in them, you'll discover what stimulates you. If you find that you just can't drag yourself to another potato chip networking event but you can't wait to get to tonight's plumbers' meeting, then go in the direction you're drawn to. Say it *is* becoming a plumber (or anything else…insert your area of interest here); the people you meet and with whom you begin to develop professional relationships will become, as I like to say, your "new best friends." Out of those relationships and the training you'll receive (because you'll want and need to learn more to participate more fully in that industry), you'll find work.

And remember: Don't worry about whether *this* opportunity is "the perfect job." Whether it is or not, you will eventually move on. Just get to work.

5.

Determine the Value of a Degree

In the 20th century, a degree was the primary, default marketing tool needed to find work. In what's become a freelance workplace in the 21st century, degrees are still necessary, but are now insufficient. A degree guarantees nothing, but you need to have one to get to the starting line.

I'm often asked by my students and clients whether they should pursue another degree. Usually my answer is yes. The more degrees you have, the more options you have. But we're predisposed to finding easy answers—rules telling us what to do, someone to do the thinking for us. You will have to choose whether a particular degree is worth the time and money you'll invest to earn it. And unfortunately, there may not be a direct correlation between the investment and the results.

When you buy a car, you know exactly what you're getting. You can choose the options you want and know ahead of time what it will feel like to drive it and how it will perform. The results of an education are more indirect. I paid approximately $70,000 for my doctorate. I can't actually measure the return on that investment, however, because it's indirect. Was it worth it? Absolutely. Can I tell you the specific results? Not exactly. I can say that since earning my doctorate, I'm smarter, I have more intellectual rigor, I am paid better for my work, and I've enjoyed teaching and publishing opportunities that I would not have had without it. Have those new opportunities paid back the $70,000? I can't say that because the opportunities were only partially as a result of my becoming Dr. Austin. The relationships I've developed, the experiences I gained, and the accomplishments I've achieved during the many years before I earned my doctorate, how I leveraged them, and my ability to market myself have all contributed—and continue to contribute—to my success.

I can't tell someone who is thinking of getting a law degree—and with it, a debt load of perhaps $100,000—whether it's going to be "worth it." What I can advise is that before you enroll in a degree program, you should decide if this degree will help you to manifest your passion in the world. In other words, don't get a law degree just because you can make more money if you have one. Don't have it be a default step because you've hit a wall in your career of choice (say, acting) and you've heard and/or read that lawyers make a lot of money, even though you're not particularly interested in the law. Instead, do your research. Talk to people who already work in the field and find out from them whether they think it's worth your time and money.

If you're just graduating college and don't want or are afraid to get into the workforce, don't get a master's degree just because you don't know exactly what you want to do. Instead, get to work. Find some kind of a job and give it a few years. You may find that you didn't need an M.B.A. after all. You might discover that you like working in art restoration, so the degree you need is an M.F.A.

6.

Understand Short-Term Thinking

The working world has changed dramatically in the past few years. It's crucial that you appreciate how these changes have affected—and will continue to affect—your potential for finding work, as well as what *types* of work you will be able to find.

A number of factors have contributed to the shift, and short-term thinking is a major one. Ever since shareholders began demanding that stock prices continually climb higher each quarter, emphasis has changed from long-term gain to short-term profitability and short-term strategies. If you run a company, you have to look for ways to increase profits at all times. The two ways to do that are to increase revenue and cut expenses.

Let's create a fictitious company. We'll call it ZYX. If you're the CEO, and ZYX is part of a mature industry in which there's little chance of increasing market share every year (let alone every quarter), your option is to cut expenses. What's the most expensive item in any company? Personnel. That's where the cutting starts.

Now say you're a ZYX employee. You may suddenly be perceived to be expendable. "But yesterday they said I was a valuable asset," you protest. Wake up. Money considerations outweigh almost everything else. The CEO is not a bad person; you'd probably behave exactly the same way in his or her position. A CEO needs to look at whether he or she can find someone who costs less to do your job. It's nothing personal. The company "cares" about you to the extent that you are an asset to it. When you begin to be perceived as a liability, you're on your way out the door.

Soon, the CEO may reasonably conclude that he or she might as well just hire people on a contract or project basis. Why should the company keep paying employees a salary when they're not busy? Why not just hire them for as long as they're needed? The production side of the entertainment industry has been using temp workers for most of its staffing needs since the studio system was dismantled beginning in the late 1940s. People are hired on an "as needed" basis, and as soon as the project is over, they're gone.

This is the landscape you face in the 21st century. The quicker—and more fully—you embrace the fact that this is the nature of the working world for the foreseeable future, the more easily you'll be able to devise a tactical approach to thriving in it.

7.

Know the Nature of the New Labor Market

Here are some of the trends that will affect your ability to find work:

- **Outsourcing.** The outsourcing industry has grown approximately 10 percent every year since 2005 and now has a market value of about $370 billion.

- **Offshoring.** An estimated 1,000,000 jobs now held by Americans will be offshored this year. That's on top of an estimated 3,000,000 manufacturing jobs that have been lost since 1998 and over 500,000 service and IT jobs that have moved overseas in recent years.

- **Temps, contract workers, and consultants**. Close to 10,000,000 people are hired in the United States every year, and only about 80 percent of them work full time.

Adding to the issue is that the power of unions has been declining. In 2012, the U.S. Bureau of Labor Statistics reported that 11.3 percent of workers were members of a union. In 1983 (the first year for which comparable data are available), the union membership rate was 20.1 percent.

If you're entering or re-entering the workforce—after losing a job, changing careers, or finishing school—these are some of the circumstances you can look forward to. Their inevitable results: downsizing, layoffs, and early retirement. Every time I read about a merger, I know the next bit of news will be that the new company is cutting its workforce. More and more workers are on their own now, and it's important that you understand this—and prepare yourself.

Remember how the very first tip in this book was "Distinguish What Is from the Way You'd Like Things to Be"? The sad truth about "what is" is that companies can show you the door at a moment's notice—often for reasons having nothing to do with your performance. Don't get too upset for too long. This is the new normal.

You are either an asset or a liability. When your employer terminates your employment and tells you "It's nothing personal," believe them. Labor costs are usually a company's biggest expense, so it's often the first thing they cut when they need to trim their budget. Like anything else—furniture, parking spaces, water coolers, etc.—you're either an asset or a liability, and you can move from one column to the other overnight.

You're like rented furniture. In the world of higher education, I call adjunct professors—who do the majority of the teaching—"migrant workers with degrees." Don't be insulted and don't fight it. Your talents are used (hopefully not misused) for as long as they're valuable to others—and then returned to where you came from when you're no longer of use.

These are the realities you need to accept to meet the challenges of the new freelance marketplace.

8.

Embrace Being a Freelancer

Corporate loyalty is becoming less and less common. Employers can't afford to care about your long-term needs. No matter how much your boss may like you; no matter how many awards, raises, and great performance reviews you've received; no matter how long you've worked there; you are expendable. And it can happen at any time—often due to factors beyond your control and despite the great job you've been doing. Don't get too comfortable.

Even if you have a full-time job, you—all of us—are a freelancer now and for the foreseeable future. A *freelancer* is "someone who sells his or her services without a long-term commitment to an employer." (Freelancing is also known as contract work, project work, temp work, or "as needed" work.) The downturn in full-time jobs with benefits makes it imperative that you start thinking of yourself as a free-lancer—sort of a discount version of a free agent in professional sports. You need to learn how to sell yourself and the services, expertise, and experience you offer.

Welcome to the 21st century. It's not fun. Get used to having two concurrent jobs: your actual job and a second job that involves marketing yourself for future work. This is what musicians and people in motion picture and television production have been doing for decades. It's now spread to virtually every other industry. The people who are the most successful are the ones who are good at the marketing job. As the expression goes, "You can't know where you're going until you know where you are." So now that you have some sense of the employment landscape, let's look at how you can successfully navigate it.

9.
Develop a New Habit

It's time for you to develop a new habit, and that habit is called "selling yourself." I am well aware that you probably don't want to be a freelancer. For most people, the thought of having to constantly sell themselves to strangers for the rest of their lives is abhorrent. "If I'd wanted to learn to freelance, constantly selling myself, I would have gone to the College of Sales." But the truth is, whatever you do, you're in sales. You don't have to like it; you just have to do it. If you have a dog, you have to pick up after the dog. Sales is like the "picking up" part that lets you enjoy the dog.

If I said to you, "Guess what? Tonight, when you get home, you'll get to brush your teeth! Doesn't that sound like fun?!" You'd reply, "Fun? Are you crazy? That's not fun! It's just a habit." Well, freelancing and selling yourself are habits, too. And the more you do them, the better you'll get.

Look, I know the advice I'm giving you won't go down easy. And I realize that a lot of what you'll read in this book runs counter to conventional wisdom. Most likely, you're at what I call a "resistance point." I'm telling you something, and you're saying, "Whoa, wait a minute! That can't be right. I can't—or won't—do that!" But I've done this work for many years and with great success. You may not believe in or want to do the things I suggest, but I promise that they work.

10.

Adapt to Technology

Technology was supposed to make us more productive—and it has. It was also supposed to allow us to have more leisure time. Well, not so much.

Are you working more but finding that you're not being paid any more than you were when you put in less time? As with a lot things in life, one thing was promised but the opposite came to pass. Smartphones, laptops, iPads, and other forms of technology have become hi-tech handcuffs (or electronic leashes, if you prefer). From a company's perspective, technology means it can get more out of its workers for less money. It's very efficient and cost-effective to have workers electronically chained and available for work 24/7.

We've gotten busier—so busy that traditional forms of communication have broken down. In the working world, that means if you're sending your résumé in response to a job posting, it's probably not getting read. You'll need to find alternative ways to connect with people you want to work for or with.

Back in the olden days—say 20 or 30 years ago—there were a couple of job titles called "Assistant" and "Secretary." These people would do grunt work for managers and executives -the typing, filing, etc. Today, thanks to technology, we're all doing that work for ourselves. And because of technology, we're available to work more hours. Employers are only too happy to take advantage of this fact—and of you.

We all are doing the work of at least two people—and your boss is, too. If you work for a company that has had layoffs and you were lucky enough to keep your job, you've now taken on the work of those who were let go. You may well be doing the work of three or four people, being paid for just one, and grateful to have a job at all!

Let's set the scene, as they say in Hollywood. Suppose an employer has a job opening and posts it. In response, 500 or 1,000 résumés will likely flood in. That figure is not an exaggeration. A colleague of mine who is an executive with the Walt Disney Company was amazed to receive 500 résumés for a single assistant position. Human Resources told him, "That's nothing. The record for a job opening at Disney is 14,000 résumés!"

I was involved in digital media for about 10 years, starting in the early 1990s—even before there was a World Wide Web. We early adopters felt that digital media would change everything, and so it has. Many things that people counted on as the foundations of their lives in the mid 20th century are becoming unrecognizable or have simply disappeared: commercial radio, newspapers, magazines, phone books, the Big Three auto makers, the dominance of the three television broadcast networks.

All of this is due to technology—and technology has changed the workplace, too. You have no choice but to adapt—or die.

11.

Increase Revenue and Cut Expenses

In the freelance world of the 21st century, in which all of us are always hustling for work, you have to begin treating yourself as a business. This is a lifelong practice. I used to say that you only have to do this until you retire, but since most of us won't be able to afford to retire, you only have to do it until you die. After that, you're off the hook.

We need to become more conscious about how to handle money. Many of us have not been trained to deal with it effectively. We don't know how to plan for the future by creating a budget—or even how to balance a checkbook. Consumer bankruptcies consistently exceed 1,000,000 every year, and the average college student is more likely to drop out of school due to financial hardship than academic failure.

There are two ways to make money: increase revenue and cut expenses. I'll begin with increasing revenue. (Reminder: Be aware of the difference between gross and net. When you earn a paycheck, you take home the net, roughly 70 percent of the gross.)

If you ran a company, would you have just one client? Of course not. If for some reason the client went under, so would your company. To protect yourself, you have multiple clients. If you consider your freelance work your "business," then ideally you want multiple ways in which to generate income, all connected to and feeding off of one another. I call this the "multiple income streams approach." If you're a visual learner, imagine spokes on a wheel with your brand at the center.

I'll use myself as an example. I'm a career mentor. That's my brand. I can derive revenue for that brand in the following ways:

- Providing career counseling for individuals
- Teaching college courses in career development
- Leading workshops
- Leading seminars
- Consulting for colleges and universities
- Authoring articles and books
- Public speaking

This logic runs counter to the 20th century idea of one job, one boss, one paycheck. But structuring your career in this way will help you survive and flourish in the new world of work.

As for reducing expenses, you need to look at the cost versus the benefit, which can be difficult to decide. For example, do you attend a networking meeting or stay home and email your client base to learn if they have any upcoming work for you? In this case, it may be a crapshoot: You might attend the meeting and find it was a waste of time. Then again, you might go to the meeting and make a contact that changes your life. You'll never know unless you go. (Sometimes you can make yourself crazy worrying about this. Just know that inevitably you will waste some of your time on meetings and proposals that yield no revenue, and that that's okay.)

Focus on distinguishing needs from wants. Think of your business as being like the human body. When you get cold, notice how it's your extremities that freeze first. That's because your body heat is being used to protect your vital organs. As the owner of your own business, your needs—your vital organs—include rent, utilities, and business supplies. Some of what you *think* are needs (that latte every morning, expensive dinners) are really wants. This becomes clear when you're forced to choose between paying the rent or going out for dinner. The truth is, you have no choice; you must do the responsible adult thing (paying the rent) and postpone the extras (going out for dinner).

Just as a car needs both an accelerator and a brake, so, too, do you—and you need to take on both roles in your own life. That means being the gas pedal to move things forward and being the brake pedal to avoid crashing into a wall. Freud called these the "id" and the "ego," respectively; you can also think of them as the child and the adult. You need to become your own parent, meaning that there are short-term wants you will need to sacrifice for the longer-term commitments you've made to manifest your talents in the world.

Lenny Bruce (1925–1966), the brilliant standup comedian, social critic, and satirist, died of a drug overdose when he was only 40. At the time, it was said that "Lenny sinned against his talent." Don't sin against the talent(s) you were given. The world needs your gifts; you have no right to be self-indulgent.

The first rule of freelancing (running your own business) is to keep your overhead low. When developing your monthly budget, be aware of the following categories of expenses, and begin to always look for ways to trim them.

- **Education (tuition, books, supplies, etc.).** Can you buy books at half price, rent them, or borrow them from your classmates?

- **Entertainment (eating out, cable, movies, concerts, theater, sporting events, downloads, apps, books, magazine subscriptions, vacations, etc.).** How often do you go out? Can you cut back? Are you watching the premium channels you're paying for? Can you look for vacation deals?

- **Food (groceries, lunches, snacks, alcohol, etc.).** Can you shop somewhere less expensive? In bulk? If you spend $10 per day for lunch five days a week, for 48 weeks a year, that's $2,400 annually. If you buy lunch one day a week and bring your lunch for the remaining days, you will save $1,920 annually. Oh, and why are you drinking so much? It's not healthy. Some of us treat our cars better than we treat our own bodies. As Shirley said to Laverne, "When are you going to start treating your body like a temple instead of an amusement park?"

- **Grooming (clothing, makeup, hair, nails, laundry, dry cleaning, etc.).** Can you buy at outlet stores? Are you addicted to designer labels? Can you have a friend do your hair? Can you do your own nails rather than go to a salon?

- **Health care (insurance, medication, gym membership, etc.).** Is there a group insurance plan offered in your field that you can join? Would it be cheaper to buy weights and use them at home rather than joining a gym?

- **Housing (rent/mortgage, insurance, utilities, cell phone, texting, Internet, cleaning service/supplies, etc.).** Can you get a roommate? Are your utility bills going up for reasons you don't understand? If so, call the company. How much are you spending on your cell phone? Can you get rid of the cleaning service and clean your own home?

- **Transportation (car payment, gas, insurance, maintenance, repairs, parking, registration, bus pass, etc.).** Is it time to get a cheaper car? Can you really afford that Mercedes?

- **Other (pets, credit card payments, interest, loans, cigarettes, birthday gifts, etc.).** Can you consolidate your credit cards? Why are you still smoking? It's expensive, and will kill you. Are you saving any money? Create a cushion for birthday gifts and emergencies.

As noted by the *Los Angeles Times* in an article called "Increasing Financial Literacy: What You Don't Know Can Hurt You":

We must learn to save and budget if we want to keep buying more stuff...We must understand the concept of compound interest—how it hurts us when we pay only the minimum on our credit card bills. We must learn that low monthly payments don't equal afford-ability. We must be aware of the seductive power of marketing and separate our wants from our needs...that brokers, bankers, and salespeople aren't necessarily our friends. We must [also] understand that opening bank accounts and establishing credit are prerequisites to success in the twenty-first century.

Review your budget every six months and trim the waste or find new sources of revenue. If and when you actually have your own business, you'll be doing that every month. Get conscious and start a new habit.

THE IMPORTANCE OF PASSION

Man's desires are limited by his perceptions; none can desire what he has not perceived.

— William Blake, Poet, Painter, and Printmaker (1757–1827)

Follow your joy.

— Joseph Campbell, Mythologist, Writer, and Lecturer (1904–1987)

Just go out there and have fun…If you're having fun, the money will come.

— Willie Mays, Baseball Player, (1931–)

Many of my clients and students get stuck in their career path because they can't figure out what it is they want to do. They think that if they can just figure out what "it" is, *then* they can get started. So they take tests—*lots* of tests—to try to find the answer.

If that's where you find yourself, consider reversing the order. Jump into an industry and see how it feels. Are you engaged? Do you feel a kinship with others in the field? Do you get excited about participating in its tasks and events? Are you satisfied at the end of the working day that you've done something useful? Do you look forward to going to work the next day and learning something new? Then keep pursuing it.

Tests are fine, as is reading about something in which you're interested. But while you can read about how to make an apple pie or watch someone else make it over and over again, you need to experience making it yourself to know what it's *really* like. To use swimming as an analogy, you can look at the water as long as you like, but you have to jump in to *feel* it. Fortunately, unlike jumping into a pool, when you jump into an industry and it doesn't work out, you won't drown. Besides, just as important as discovering what you *do* want to do is learning what you *don't* want to do. Better to try something and find it wasn't for you than to look back years later with regret. ("I always wanted to try being a _____. I wish I had. Now I'll never know.") What you think you really want to do may *not* be the right career path for you. As Garth Brooks sings, "Some of God's greatest gifts are unanswered prayers."

Don't get paralyzed into inaction either because you're not sure what you want to do or because you're afraid to go after what you think you've always wanted to do. Stop overthinking. From my perspective, well into my sixth (or is it seventh?) career, we have little idea of what—or how many—careers we're going to have. Get in the game and be open to what may come.

12.
Start at the End

One of the courses I teach is critical thinking. But when *I* teach it, it's called "Critical Thinking *and* Action." Being aware of something isn't enough. You must *do* something. It's not enough to say, "After many years of therapy, I've learned that my mother was neurotic. If she hadn't been neurotic, my life wouldn't be such a mess and I'd be able to do what I've always dreamed of doing." Or, "I feel so badly for the poor, starving children in Africa." You must *do* something about those problems.

If you don't do something, it doesn't mean anything. Intention, good will, or feeling badly about something doesn't accomplish a thing. It's not what you think or how you feel; it's what you *do* that matters. (In the same way, I believe that thinking of something or even talking about doing something isn't wrong. You can be angry at someone and think, "I could *kill* him"—and haven't we all felt that way about someone at some point in our lives?—but that's not the same thing as actually committing homicide.)

The first thing to look at is, what's your goal? What's the end point? That may seem like an odd place to start, but it puts everything into focus. If you know what you want, you can then determine the steps you need to take to get there. And if you want it badly enough—and given we're talking about your career, presumably you *will* want it badly enough—you will push through whatever barriers you need to in order to get there.

What do you want to do? What's your passion—that thing you love to do for hours on end that you can get lost in, that puts you "in the zone," that makes you forget to eat or causes you to lose track of time? As Confucius said, "I am a person who forgets his food when engaged in vigorous pursuit of something." Your passion is the wellspring of how you'll shape your career.

You may have tried to determine your passion before, only to end up frustrated ("I just can't figure out what I want to do!"). If you don't know exactly what your passion is, *don't worry about it.* Spending a lot of time trying to figure out exactly what it is you want to do, what you are meant to do, or what you are supposed to do is a waste of time. I know I differ from a lot of career coaches in this regard, people like Dick Bolles, author of *What Color Is Your Parachute,* and fans of the Myers-Briggs Personality Test and others like it. But the truth is, the new normal is that you'll have multiple careers—in fact, it's predicted that Millennials will have five or six of them! Because you will most likely have more than one career, the best way to find them is through the experience of working at things you enjoy or in which you think you may be interested. You will find your passion or passions eventually. Meanwhile, get to work and do something that interests you.

13.

Don't Worry If You Don't Know What Your Passion Is

It's okay if you don't know what your passion is. I give you permission to not know. I realize you may feel pressured by (pick one or more) your parents, your friends, what you read, and so on to know what it is you want to do with your life. But it's not a law of nature that you have to know this. Stop worrying about it. Pick something you *think* you'd like to do and get to work. You'll learn on the job whether or not it's a good fit for you.

There are exercises you can do to help you figure out what your passion is, and I use them in my courses. It's more effective, however, to explore the fields in which you're interested, meet people who work in them, and get involved. That can mean job shadowing, taking workshops, volunteering, doing internships, and ultimately finding paid work. Along the way, you'll discover whether this is your calling.

14.

Find Your Passion

How will you know when you've found your passion? When you'll do whatever you have to do to succeed at it. (*You* get to define what "success" is.) Say the field you've chosen is growing fast in China and they're hiring there. If this is your passion, then you need to learn Mandarin and move to China. (You always have to go where the work is.) "But I'm no good at languages," you say. Well, my response is, how badly do you want it? Enough to push through whatever fears or preconceived ideas you may have?

I grew up in Manhattan. There was a taxi, bus, or subway within a block of virtually every street, and my family didn't own a car. So I didn't need a great sense of direction—and then decided I didn't *have* one. As an adult, I visited my mother's hometown of Antwerp, Belgium. I had to get there at night and didn't speak the language. I found my way around. I was determined. I discovered I had a *fine* sense of direction. This works for anything you want to do in life. You can push through virtually any barrier if you're committed to making something happen.

The following tips contain visualization exercises designed to enable you to determine what it is you really love to do that can be offered as a paid service to others. They were inspired by a book by Mark Pope, Carole Minor, and Tracy M. Lara called *Experiential Activities for Teaching Career Counseling Classes and for Facilitating Career Groups* published by the National Career Development Association in 2000. Presumably, after doing these exercises, you will have a good idea of a monetizeable passion—or at least a better sense of what career path to pursue.

15.

Your Dream Vacation

You have won an all expense paid vacation to the destination of your choice anywhere on the planet. You may bring a travel companion, if you wish. Where would you go? Why did you choose that place? Have you been here before? Are you alone, or did you decide to bring someone with you? If you brought someone, why did you choose that person? Picture yourself—or you and your companion—relaxing and enjoying the sites. Then consider the following:

- The destination you chose symbolizes your future careers.

- Your travel companion (or lack of one) symbolizes the types of people you want to work with.

- The transportation you use and the accommodations you have symbolize future work environments.

16.

Career Fantasies

When you were a kid, you likely fantasized about what you wanted to do when you grew up. Odds are, you imagined things like being a firefighter, a ballet dancer, a cowboy, a cowgirl, an astronaut, a doctor, etc.

Remember your first "career fantasy." Starting there, move forward in time and recall every career fantasy you ever had—lawyer, corporate executive, explorer, whatever. Picture yourself doing each one of them. Create a list of the names of these fantasy occupations.

Finally, review your list, paying special attention to the following:

- **Patterns you detected:** Leading people, creating something new, building things, overcoming physical challenges, etc.

- **Desirable features:** Working independently during the hours of your choice, being considered an expert in your field, etc.

- **The environments in which you'd work if you performed those jobs:** Traveling all over the world, working in a busy office, facing dangers in the outdoors, etc.

Notice what you're drawn to—what gives you pleasure and satisfaction.

17.

What Matters to You

Suppose you are given $1 billion, tax free. Budget your windfall according to what you value most. Following are your choices, along with what each choice symbolizes.

- Being elected to a leadership position (professional recognition)

- The elimination of inequality in the world (social justice)

- A complete library of the great books of the world, including personal access to all the people who wrote them, whether living or dead (wisdom)

- The perfect professional or romantic relationship (intimate relationship)

- Perfect health and fitness until you're 100 years old (health and long life)

- Recognition as the greatest artistic genius of your time, in your choice of any field of art (creativity)

- The perfect work environment and the job of your choice (freedom and personal autonomy)

- Travel to anywhere in the world with passes to any and all activities (adventure and risk-taking)

- True understanding of the meaning of life and the achievement of perfect harmony with all things (inner peace and spiritual harmony)

- Reaching the pinnacle of success in your chosen career field (sense of accomplishment)

- Removal of any and all threats to world peace (world peace)

- A close group of loyal friends for the rest of your life (friendship)

- A world in which everyone does things the right way (consistency and order)

- A family that's always loving and living in perfect harmony (family, affection, support, and security)

- Becoming the richest person in the world (financial security and economic independence)

- A lifetime pass to the ultimate luxury resort, where all your needs are met (leisure and comfort)

- The ability to always speak and hear the truth (honesty)

- Always being in a position to improve other's lives (service to others)

- Being aware that you can always do and be whatever you want (self-confidence)

- Achieving all your goals as a result of your hard work (self-discipline)

4

THE EMPLOYER'S
PERSPECTIVE

The customer is the most important part of the production line.

—W. Edwards Deming, Statistician, Professor, Author,
Lecturer, and Consultant (1900–1993)

The customer is the person who pays. As such, it's important to learn to empathize with your customer. In retail, that customer is the shopper. But in your case, your customer is your employer. You always want to keep your eye on your employer's needs and concerns.

Remember the Golden Rule. I don't mean the one that says, "Treat others as you'd like others to treat you" (although that's important, too). In business, the Golden Rule is, "Whoever has the gold makes the rules." An employer is someone who is trading his or her money for your skills, knowledge, network, and talents (and perhaps your creativity, if you're lucky). You want to understand that person's needs and what you can do for him. In an interview, *he* is who really matters.

You are of service to the employer. You need to be the person who "rides to the rescue" like the U.S. Cavalry always did in old Western movies. You need to reassure the employer that if he places you in a role, with a minimum amount of supervision and time, you can fix his problem. Your role is to take work away from the employer, to handle something he needs handled, which will allow him to move on to something else without having to worry about whether what he hired you to do is getting done.

18.

Identify What Employers Are Looking For

I am a college professor, an author, a career counselor—and a boss. As a boss, when I hire people, I look for the following:

- Someone who fills most or all of the three or four key requirements for the job.

- A referral from someone whose judgment I trust. This tells me you're someone who's been vetted and can do the job.

- A well-written résumé that's professional both in content and presentation, clear, and to the point. This will indicate your experience and suitability for the position.

- Good follow-up throughout the process, including the following:

  - Did the candidate confirm the interview in a well-written email?

  - Did he or she bring the materials I requested to the interview?

  - Did the candidate arrive early?

  - Is he or she appropriately dressed?

  - Did the candidate offer a firm handshake and a smile?

  - Did I get a thank-you after the interview?

  - Did the candidate supply any additional materials I requested in a timely manner?

  - Did the candidate behave professionally throughout the entire process?

In other words, it's not just about the interview itself; it's the entire process that gives the employer a sense of whether you're a professional.

When I conduct an interview, my entire team is present. This is similar to the increasingly popular "panel interview." After all, the new member has to work with all of us, and we all have to want them to join us. The interview should close the deal by making me—and my team—fairly certain that you'll be a good fit. Here's what they look for:

- Is this person someone I'd want to live with? (We spend more of our waking time with people with whom we work than we do with our loved ones!)

- Is this person likable and upbeat?

- Is this person intelligent and articulate?

One more thing: Whether you're friendly and someone I want to spend time with—in other words, your personality—is becoming increasingly important.

19.

Know Who Matters

In an interview, the only person who truly matters is the one doing the hiring. Your job is to make that person comfortable with the idea of having you join her team. So you want to thoroughly research the company. Learn what it does and what it's planning—and how you can help it achieve those goals.

Take the attention away from yourself and your needs and focus on what you can do for the people you're talking to. Talin Koutnouyan, with whom I worked at Woodbury University, explained what a difference this "service" approach made for her:

After I shifted my way of thinking, I walked into every interview giving off the vibe that I was there to serve and exert all my effort for them. Today, I got a call telling me I had three offers from three different interviews. Not only that, but since all of the employers I had interviewed with were aware of the number of offers I had, I chose the position that best matched my skills and had the most competitive pay of the three.

20.

Prepare for the Right Questions

Practice interviewing over and over again to become comfortable fielding answers to questions you can expect to hear in a formal interview. Following are some of these questions, and guidelines on how to answer them.

- **Tell me about yourself. What adjectives would you or your friends use to describe you?** Before you answer this question, get clarification. Ask, "What specifically in my résumé stood out that you would like me to talk about?" This will help you direct the interview. When the employer responds to this question, you will be able to focus your answer on what the interviewer is looking for.

- **What are your greatest strengths?** Given that an interview is essentially a business meeting, you can reasonably assume that the interviewer is interested in strengths that apply to his bottom line. In other words, "I'm an excellent windsurfer" is probably not the best response. Instead, mention things like your ability to generate new business, your strong work ethic, and your creativity in finding solutions that aren't apparent at first glance.

- **What do you consider your greatest accomplishment?** Provide an answer that applies to your career. If you don't have a lot of work experience, talk about your accomplishments in school. If you've raised children—your own or your siblings — you can use that. Some of the best office managers are parents who have returned to the workforce after raising their families; a hiring manager will appreciate that you can easily deal with the "children" in the office. (I have friend who is a therapist. A great many of his patients are C-level executives. He says they behave just like children on a playground. The only difference is that they're wearing suits.)

41

- **What is your biggest weakness? Name two things you'd like to improve about yourself.** People are invariably perplexed about how to answer this question. They want to be honest, but they don't want to expose any weakness. Just know that in interviews, there is the question you're being asked, and then there's the *real* question, known as the "metaquestion." The interviewer *seems* to be asking you to make yourself vulnerable by confessing a shortcoming. But what she *actually* wants to know is whether you have learned to identify and manage your lesser qualities. Thus, the way to answer this question is to state the "weakness" ("I'm a workaholic."), and then how you've learned to manage it ("What I've learned is that after 12 or 14 hours, I run out of steam. So I quit for the day, get a good night's sleep, and am ready to go full steam ahead the next morning."). This tells the interviewer three things: (1) You're self-reflective and honest about your limitations. (2) You're a workaholic. (This is a good thing in the business world.) (3) You're a managed workaholic. You've learned to successfully deal with problems. The assumption is that if you can manage yourself, you may be able to manage others.

- **How do your co-workers and friends describe you? What would they say you need to improve?** This is another version of the preceding question, only this time you also get to say some positive things about yourself.

- **Are you a team player? Give some examples.** Your answer should include how you put the team's needs above your own.

- **Describe a time when you worked with someone "difficult."** What happened, and how did you resolve the problem? To answer this question, first outline what happened. Then describe how you took action. Finally, explain the result, which should involve some improvement in the situation.

- **Why did you leave your last job (or why are you leaving your current job)?** I'll answer this by telling you what *not* to do: Don't trash your last employer. In fact, never say anything bad about anyone. It may well come back to bite you. At the very least, it makes you look like a whiner or a victim. No one wants to be around that kind of person.

- **What would you like to be doing one/five/10 years from now?** If you're young, you may not have any idea. That's okay. You're not under oath, so you don't have to commit to what you say. What the interviewer *really* wants to know is if you're ambitious (but not too ambitious) and forward-thinking. So your answer could be something like, "I see myself becoming the CEO of this company or one like it." Or, "Someday I'd like to run my own business in this industry."

- **If you were an animal, what animal would you be?** Yes, they really ask this question. Why? To throw you off balance. In class, a male student of mine once answered honestly, "A soft pussycat." This might not be the best answer. My advice? Try to match the animal to the kind of job for which you're applying. For a sales job, they want someone who's quick and aggressive, like a cheetah or a shark. For a senior management position, perhaps you'd be an elephant or a lion.

- **If you were part of a salad, what part would you be?** (Variations to this question include, "If you could be any superhero, who would you be, and why?" and "What color best represents your personality?") Here, you would offer the same type of answer as with the previous question. If the job for which you're applying requires something bold, you might go with a zesty dressing. If sharpness is what's needed, you might answer, "Parmesan cheese."

(Are you beginning to understand why it's so much easier to develop relationships with people beforehand, so you can avoid the formal interview and these sorts of silly questions?)

21.

Answer These Questions

Now that you've gotten some practice providing answers that your potential employer wants to hear, try your hand at these:

- What got you interested in what you do? Why did you choose to do what you do?

- What makes you a good candidate for this job?

- What new skills have you recently developed?

- How do you handle deadlines?

- How do you balance your priorities?

- How do you deal with criticism?

- How do you deal with stress?

- Give me an example of a time you failed.

- Give me an example of a time you showed leadership.

- Why should we hire you? What unique qualities or abilities would you bring to this job that would make you successful?

- Give me an example of a time you had to be creative to solve a problem at work.

- Give me an example of a time you persuaded or influenced a group of people.

- Tell me about your most difficult boss. How was he or she difficult? How did you deal with him or her?

- Why is there a gap in your résumé?

- How does your previous experience relate to this position?

- Why do you want to work here? What do you know about this company?

- Tell me about your experience at your college or university. Why did you choose to attend that school?

- What was your favorite class in school, and why? What was your most challenging class in school, and why?

- What are you passionate about?

- Tell me about one of your most creative moments, either professional or personal.

- What are the most rewarding aspects of a job for you?

- What successful people in your field inspire you, and why?

- Sell me on my company or product.

- What are your pet peeves?

- What does success mean to you?

- If you felt any weakness pertaining to this job, what would it be?

- What has been your biggest career-related crisis?

- What are the things that motivate you?

- Describe your ideal job.

- At what point did you choose this career?

- What motivates you to put forth your greatest effort?

- Give examples of experiences at school or in a job that were satisfying. Give examples of experiences that were dissatisfying.

- Provide examples to convince me that you can adapt to a wide variety of people, situations, and environments.

- Tell me about a time you had to juggle multiple responsibilities. How did you organize the work?

- Tell me about a time you had to make a decision but didn't have all the information you needed.

- Give an example of something you did to build enthusiasm in others.

- Give an example of a time when someone you worked with criticized you in front of others. What was your response?

- Give an example of a time you had to sell a supervisor on a concept or idea. What steps did you take? Did you win?

Practice your answers to each of these questions. Among the most important and useful exercises in my career courses and workshops are the mock interview. Mock interviews provide an opportunity to rehearse and refine your answers. And because they take place in a safe environment where there's no downside to giving the wrong answer, the stress of interviewing is reduced. The more time you invest in learning to handle these questions, the more your answers will become muscle memory and the more comfortable you'll be if and when you ever need to participate in a formal interview.

5

COMMUNICATION

There is no magic, only brute persistence, consistency, and attention to detail.

—Tom Peters, Business Management Practices Author (1942–)

S kills and talent are insufficient for success. You need a combination of skills, talent, and drive—*and* the ability to communicate them.

Madonna is a good example of this. Is she a great singer? Probably no one would say that. But she's a good enough singer, and combined with her songwriting, production skills, and drive, plus her ability to communicate—to connect with—her audience, that's been enough to enable her to become enormously successful.

This chapter deals with the communication part of self-promotion— both verbal and written—and how a disciplined approach to both can create the desired impact on your audience.

22.

Write for Business

It's become common practice to blame the Internet for the fact that many Americans—particularly Millennials—have underdeveloped communication skills. But while our addiction to Twitter and texting are contributing factors, the point here is not to blame, but to fix.

When it comes to communication, I believe most of us were mis-taught during elementary, middle, and high school. If you're like me, you were given writing assignments that focused on gross tonnage versus content. "Give me 10 pages on [a topic that had little relevance to your own life]," your teacher would say. Or, "Your assignment is 500 words on [another topic of virtually no interest to you]." You then wrote the paper by cutting and pasting information from other sources (i.e., plagiarizing), padding it so you could reach the required number of words or pages. You didn't read it over or edit it. You just handed it in. It was an assignment you tossed off as quickly as you could because you didn't care. The faster you got it done, the faster you could get to some other activity that *did* interest you. Writing became a chore—something to get out of the way—and the connection between writing and communicating was broken.

I teach writing (or more accurately, re-teach it or un-teach it). The writing I teach, which is writing for business, consists of two simple concepts:

- What are you trying to say?
- Who's your audience?

When you write for business (and in your case, writing for the purpose of finding work), you want to operate counterintuitively from how you were taught in school. Rather than padding a paper on a topic that means nothing to you, you want to use as *few* words as possible to communicate with people who can refer you or hire you, whether it's a cover letter, résumé, thank-you note, or follow-up email. As Thomas Jefferson said, "The most valuable of all talents is that of never using two words when one will do."

Just as when you interview, when you write to someone, you need to respect his or her time and needs. People are busy, so you need to come to the point quickly. Imagine you're being charged $5 for every extra word you use; that might help you learn to edit!

Speaking of editing, writing *is* editing. Think of editing as being like rehearsing. Does an actor perform the first rehearsal of a monologue she has to deliver to a paid audience? Of course not. She practices over and over again until it's ready for the public. You want to do the same for any communications that have your name on them. Write them over and over again until they're ready to go. Remember: You don't have the luxury of having the person to whom you're writing— your boss, hiring manager, or whoever—ask you to explain what you meant to say. You have one chance to nail it, so take as much time as you need so the final product you send is perfect.

Speaking as an employer, I want to read a résumé that is error-free and accurately represents what you can deliver, an email in which you've told me exactly what it is you want me to know, etc.

Here's a great tip: Always read whatever you've written out loud. It may read beautifully on the page or screen, but you will often discover that what you meant to say isn't what you wrote.

In that case, go back and fix it. I'm a published author and I do this all the time. You should, too. Unlike the papers you wrote in school, these cover letters, résumés, and other communications matter to you—because they will help you find work.

23.

Improve Your Verbal Presentation Skills

Polls have shown that people would rather die than speak in public. I also teach speaking (both my writing and speaking courses are "wing" courses to my career development course). If you can't communicate well, both in writing and verbally, your résumé isn't going to get you where you want to go. The hard skills—that is, your specific talents and abilities—get you in; but your soft skills—i.e., communication—move you up.

I don't teach public speaking, because that term implies that you're going to be speaking to large groups. Most of us never will. Besides, I can't turn you into a Barack Obama or Rev. Martin Luther King, Jr. in an 11- or 15-week course. I'm an educator, not a magician. What I teach is speaking to one other person or to small groups because this is what you'll have to do in the business world—think interviews or presentations.

Here's a tip: Focus on the concept of contribution. You have something valuable to contribute to your audience. You need to push past whatever shyness or anxiety you may have to get the message across. It's not about you; it's about them and their needs. (Sound familiar?) Whatever detracts from conveying that message needs to be eliminated—think verbal hiccups like "y'know," "uh," "like," etc.

Verbal presentation is about the steak and the sizzle. The "steak" is the content. You need to fully research your topic so you are an authority on the subject (or at least more authoritative than your audience). The "sizzle" is how you present your topic, the show. People like to be entertained and stimulated. You need to get their attention and connect your content to their needs. Consciously or not, they are thinking, "Why should I care about this?" Unless you can connect with them and explain why they should care about what you're telling them, they won't listen.

24.
Read

What do the people who work in your field read to stay current on trends? You need to be reading the same publications. It's surprising how many job seekers don't do this. If I'm interviewing you, I want to know that you're aware of trends, changes, and forecasts. This is how I know we speak the same language and that you'll fit in with my team. Immerse yourself in our world.

There are other benefits to keeping current on what's happening in your industry. Years ago, I was interested in working in the music business, so I started reading its bible, *Billboard*. Each issue featured a column called "Executive Roundtable," which covered personnel changes in the field. I read it regularly.

At the time, my daughter, Monique, was an *au pair* for the daughter of a couple we knew, Jeff and Melody. Jeff worked at Epic Records. One Monday, the "Executive Roundtable" column noted that Jeff's assistant, Connie, was taking a leave of absence. I immediately called Jeff and asked him if he'd thought of a replacement for Connie. He said he hadn't yet—and wondered if I'd be interested in the job. I was. I went in to see him, and the job was mine!

As you get more involved in your field, you'll meet more people. Industries are fluid. Companies change ownership, expand, and contract. New companies are formed. People move around. As you're looking for opportunities, you'll begin to see more and more people you know who are starting companies or getting promoted.

Your next job or project could be a phone call away. It might go something like this:

You: "Mary! How are you? I just read in [insert industry publication] that you've been named to start a new division of your company. Congratulations!"

Mary: "How thoughtful of you to call! Your timing's great. I remember when we had lunch a couple of weeks ago that you said were now specializing in [insert your newly acquired skill]. I'm staffing up and need someone who can do this. Would you have some time at 4 o'clock this afternoon to come in and meet with me about it?"

Yes, it can be that easy—because you've laid the groundwork. Luck, as they say, is the residue of design.

25.

Establish and Develop Your Brand

When you think of Coca-Cola, what comes to mind?

- Brown

- Bubbly

- Sweet

- Refreshing

- Caffeine kick

- Carbonated

That's Coke's brand. A *brand*—whether it's yours, Coca-Cola's, Apple's, Google's, or anybody else's—is the relationship between you and your audience. How does your consumer (or market or fan base) think and feel about you and your skills, abilities, and experience? What's your reputation?

Your brand is a list of specific marketable and transferable skills that you can monetize. What I'm talking about are hard skills, like the languages you speak, the software programs with which you're proficient, the quantifiable results you've attained for other companies. I stress "specific skills" because I've seen far too many résumés listing soft skills like "good team player," "able to work independently," and "good oral and written communication skills." These are too general, and they're a given for someone who has a degree. In other words, what distinguishes you? What makes you stand out from the competition? What makes your brand unique? As an employer who may be willing to pay you, what exactly are you going to be able to do for me?

That's not to say those "soft skills" aren't part of your brand, too. When your market thinks of you, what comes to mind?

- Creative
- Good follow-through
- Friendly
- Team player
- Hardworking
- Quick learner
- Good attitude

Or is it:

- Flaky
- Drama queen (this can apply to any gender)
- Difficult
- Full of excuses
- Unreliable

The impression people have of you is what will get you work. If Helen is seen as a good team player—someone who is reliable, hardworking, creative, and positive—then when colleagues ask about her, they'll find she's someone they would want to work with.

Put yourself in the hiring manager's shoes. You make inquiries to trusted colleagues about another candidate (let's call him Todd). The word on Todd is that he's a whiner—a prima donna, unreliable, someone with a bad attitude. Would you hire him? No. You'd hire Helen. Be like Helen.

26.

Articulate Your Brand

Let's work on how to state your attributes. This applies to when you're speaking about yourself or creating your résumé. For example:

■ Fluent in Spanish, Mandarin, and English.

"Fluent" means you can speak, read, and write in the language. "Business fluent," as I describe it, means that if an employer hires you and puts you on the phone with a client in Shanghai, you know Mandarin well enough to close the deal.

■ Proficient in Abode Illustrator, Adobe Photoshop, and Quick-Books.

Add whatever software is specific to the field in which you work—or the field in which you *want* to work. The first programs you list should be those of most value to the people in that field. Microsoft Office should come last because you're *supposed* to know it and almost everyone does (unless of course you're applying for an office job where MS Office will be the program you primarily use). Say "proficient" instead of "knowledgeable," as the employer is not interested in what you know but in what you can do for his or her company.

■ Produced at least a 10% annual increase in sales for the last two companies for which I worked.

When you speak—or write—about yourself, avoid generalities. Focus on the following:

■ What you do.

■ What you've accomplished. People are not that interested in how hard you worked or the process you followed.

■ What quantifiable results you achieved—and how they affected the bottom line.

Business people want to make money. How you can help them do that is less about what you know (your education) and more about what you can do (your work experience). I will always choose an experienced professional over someone who's studied something but not actually done it. After all, who would you rather hire? A chef— or someone who has read a cookbook? Remember: The combination of skills, experience, and performance you offer is unique in the world. I have worked with hundreds of people over the years and have yet to find two who were exactly alike.

Your brand—your reputation—always precedes you. When you're being considered for work, it's what people think, remember, and say about you that determines whether you'll get a meeting.

While I was working with a film production company, the producer, Jim, and the director, Debbie, were talking about editors they might want to work with. Soon, Ralph's name came up. Their conversation about him was brief:

Jim: "What about Ralph for the editor's job?"

Debbie: "No. He's a pain."

Needless to say, Ralph was never interviewed.

Often it's unconscious, but the people who meet you, spend time with you, work with you—your family members, friends, and co-workers— are always cataloguing your behaviors. While friends and family are more forgiving, the impression you make determines how willing others will be to put in a good word for you, recommend you, or provide you with leads in the future.

Make sure that anyone you spend time with has a good feeling about you. They won't stick their necks out for someone who may embarrass them in front of a business associate and close off that relationship for themselves. Like it or not, you're always on display, always auditioning, and must always be "on." You're always performing.

27.

Identify Your Unique Selling Proposition (USP)

"Unique selling proposition"—USP for short—is a marketing term that will help you define the unique qualities of your brand (versus the competition). Your USP may be only a matter of how you're perceived, but given that some people believe perception *is* reality, that's okay. Is one brand of beer "better" than another? Depends on who you ask. What's important for the beer company is that the consumer *perceives* that it is.

When you're marketing your brand, what the people in your industry think of you—your reputation—is sometimes all you need to get the work. I've hired people because other people I trust have vouched for them; the interview simply confirmed what I was predisposed to believe.

In an interview, you need to convey your USP—the combination of qualities that separates you from the competition—to help explain why I should hire you.

The question is, then, how do you identify your USP? That's where your résumé comes in. Your résumé is really the script for your pitch, and identifying your USP is really just a residual benefit of having crafted a résumé that really represents what you offer. The first thing to look at—always—is, who is your audience? Then ask yourself, what does your audience need you to be? Highlight the key qualities that make you *you* in the marketplace.

When I had a consultancy in digital media doing marketing and business development, some of my clients asked me to create company descriptions to post on Google and Yahoo!. Those sites required descriptions as short as 10 words. My first response was, "I can't possibly describe what this company does in 10 words!" You may feel the same way when you're trying to reduce your résumé to a few words. Guess what? You can. Now go through it again and eliminate any extraneous words.

28.

Develop Your Sound Bite, or Elevator Pitch

Test the USP you've created on friends and colleagues to see if it resonates with them. When you feel it's polished, start using it when you're meeting new people in your field. (Don't be afraid to alter it slightly, depending on the person to whom you're speaking.) Now you have your sound bite, or elevator pitch.

To give you an example, my sound bite might be, "I'm Chaz Austin, or 'Dr. Chaz' as my students call me. I'm an author and a college professor specializing in training my clients and students for the workplace." Again, it's okay to alter your sound bite. For example, if I'm speaking to someone in academia, I would probably mention the teaching first. I'm trying to get them interested, so I'm looking at what *they* would care about most.

The good news is, just as with your writing, you get to practice your sound bite over and over again until it works. Eventually, you will get comfortable saying it whenever someone asks you what it is you do.

Your sound bite is your primary marketing tool. It's how most people will first be introduced to you. If they like what they hear, it will create the opportunity for further conversation, referrals, etc. Be aware that it will change over time as the focus of your career changes and as you add new skills and experiences.

If all this feels overwhelming, be patient. Remember that you're developing a new habit, and developing anything takes time. It's a process. You *will* get better at doing this. Your goal is not to be a great salesperson, nor is it to enjoy the sales process. (That's probably not going to happen.) Rather, your goal is to be just good enough at it to keep getting work. And that's worth the trouble—and the practice.

29.

Prepare for the Audition

Not only do you have sell yourself in 21st century America, you have to do it *all the time*. You're always "on." Every interaction is an opportunity to show yourself in a good light. You never know who knows someone who knows someone who might want to hire you. Marketing yourself is a full-time job. Remember, I didn't say you'd necessarily like it. But it will get you to a place where you can do what you love. Isn't that worth it?

A few years ago, I was visiting my fiancé (now my wife) in New York City over the Christmas holidays. She owned two dogs, who had to be walked every morning and evening. New York can be really cold in late December, and that year was no exception. Although I grew up there, I've lived in Los Angeles for many years and no longer deal very well with cold weather. But I loved my fiancé, and her dogs (who later became *our* dogs when we got married) needed to go out…at 6:00 a.m.!

I put on every piece of warm clothing I'd brought with me and out we went to the dog park (which, in Manhattan, is essentially a slab of concrete surrounded by a chain link fence). When we arrived, there was one other hapless dog owner there—Laura Morrison, an acquaintance of my fiancé's. We got to talking and it turned out that she was a writer doing a piece for the online version of the *Wall Street Journal* on the subject of—wait for it—finding work! I told her what I did and handed her a business card. A few weeks later her piece appeared—and it included quotes from me!

The moral of the story is, you never know when a networking opportunity may occur, so always have your business cards with you and be ready to pitch yourself.

RÉSUMÉS AND COVER LETTERS

Emphasize your strengths on your résumé, in your cover letters, and in your interviews. It may sound obvious, but you'd be surprised how many people simply list everything they've ever done. Convey your passion and link your strengths to measurable results. Employers and interviewers love concrete data.

—Marcus Buckingham, Author, Researcher, Motivational Speaker, and Business Consultant (1966–)

Way back in the 20th century, résumés were the most important tool for finding a job. That's not so much the case nowadays. However, they are still useful and necessary, and can serve as a dynamic marketing tool. This chapter will explore how to use them, what belongs in them, and what doesn't.

30.

Use Your Résumé as a Marketing Document

Your résumé is not a history of everything you've done in your career. Employers and hiring managers are really only interested in what you've accomplished that will help make (or save) them money. Rather, your résumé is a marketing document that shows you in the best possible light. Think of it as being like makeup. It should accentuate your best features while hiding your flaws. If you have a big nose, there are ways to apply your makeup to either accentuate the size of your nose or to try to hide it. Either way, you still have a big nose—but with the right makeup, you can play it down.

Never lie on your résumé, however. But it's okay to omit certain experiences that would be of no importance to the employer. I played the drums for 15 years, but that fact never appears on my résumé—unless I'm applying to teach a college music course. (I've taught "The History of Rock 'n' Roll" and "Music and Society.") Always look to the needs of the employer first.

31.
Include the Right Information

Here's what goes on your résumé, in this order:

- Your name
- Your contact information, including your street address, phone number, professional email address, and any websites that give the employer a more robust picture of who you are, what you do, and what you have accomplished
- Your objective and anything that directly supports it, such as languages, software programs, and so on in which you're fluent

Then what? Do you put your education or your work experience next? It depends on what's stronger. When you're on a first date, don't you emphasize the things that are most impressive about you first? Of course you do, because you're trying to make a good first impression. Your résumé is often your first impression in a business setting. Lead with your strengths.

32.
One or Two Pages?

For some strange reason, the length of a résumé has become a source of anxiety among job seekers. Generally, if you've worked for 10 years or less, one page should suffice. If you have more than 10 years of experience, then it ought to be two pages long. Notice I said generally. If you want to know what's appropriate in your specific field, ask. Talk to people you know in your field. Also, contact the human resources departments of the companies for which you're interested in working and find out what they prefer.

33.
Appeal to Your Audience

Should you have a separate résumé for every job you apply for? No. Having a different résumé for every job you apply for is going to make you crazy. That being said, you may want to have two different résumés if you have two separate careers. Take me, for example. I'm both a career counselor and a professor, so two different résumés would be appropriate. It's all about your audience. In my case, I'm appealing to two different ones: school administrators in the first case and department chairs in the second.

To facilitate this, consider creating your résumé in Microsoft Word or a similar word-processing program. That way, it will be easy to move the various modules around to suit the needs of the particular job for which you're applying.

34.

Less Is More

Creating a one- or two-page résumé forces you to use the fewest possible words to describe exactly what you have accomplished.

Employers like action verbs, so use them. Doing so will help you to get to the heart of what it is you did—and what you can presumably deliver for your next employer—in as few words as possible. Table 6.1 includes several strong action words that pertain to a variety of skills.

Table 6.1—Action Verbs

Management Skills

Administered	Analyzed	Assigned	Attained	Chaired	Consolidated
Contracted	Coordinated	Delegated	Developed	Directed	Evaluated
Executed	Improved	Increased	Organized	Oversaw	Planned
Prioritized	Produced	Recommended	Reviewed	Scheduled	Strengthened
Supervised					

Communication Skills

Addressed	Arbitrated	Arranged	Authored	Collaborated	Convinced
Corresponded	Developed	Directed	Drafted	Edited	Enlisted
Formulated	Influenced	Interpreted	Lectured	Mediated	Moderated
Negotiated	Persuaded	Promoted	Publicized	Reconciled	Recruited
Spoke	Translated	Wrote			

Research Skills

Clarified	Collected	Critiqued	Diagnosed	Evaluated	Examined
Extracted	Identified	Inspected	Interpreted	Interviewed	Investigated
Organized	Reviewed	Summarized	Surveyed	Systematized	

Technical Skills

Assembled	Built	Calculated	Computed	Designed	Devised
Engineered	Fabricated	Maintained	Operated	Overhauled	Programmed
Remodeled	Repaired	Solved	Upgraded		

Teaching Skills

Adapted	Advised	Clarified	Coached	Communicated	Coordinated
Demystified	Developed	Enabled	Encouraged	Evaluated	Explained
Facilitated	Guided	Informed	Instructed	Persuaded	Set goals
Stimulated	Trained				

Financial Skills

Administered	Allocated	Analyzed	Appraised	Audited	Balanced
Budgeted	Calculated	Computed	Developed	Forecasted	Managed
Marketed	Planned	Projected	Researched		

Creative Skills

Acted	Conceptualized	Created	Customized	Designed	Developed
Directed	Established	Fashioned	Founded	Illustrated	Initiated
Instituted	Integrated	Introduced	Invented	Originated	Performed
Planned	Revitalized	Shaped			

Helping Skills

Assessed	Assisted	Clarified	Coached	Counseled	Demonstrated
Diagnosed	Educated	Expedited	Facilitated	Familiarized	Guided
Motivated	Referred	Rehabilitated	Represented		

Clerical or Detail Skills

Approved	Arranged	Catalogued	Classified	Collected	Compiled
Dispatched	Executed	Generated	Implemented	Inspected	Monitored
Operated	Organized	Prepared	Processed	Purchased	Recorded
Retrieved	Screened	Specified	Systematized	Tabulated	Validated

Other Verbs

Achieved	Expanded	Improved	Pioneered	Reduced	Resolved
Restored	Spearheaded	Transformed			

35.

Include an Objective in Your Résumé...For Now

Should you include an "objective" in your résumé? There is no absolute answer. It's all a matter of what's currently popular. At the moment, however, most employers want an objective, so you should include one.

While you don't have to customize your whole résumé for each job, you can—and probably should—customize your objective to reflect the specific job or assignment you're pursuing.

When I hire, I read (or, more accurately, scan) each résumé from the top down. If I see that the job seeker is going after a position that isn't the one for which I'm hiring, I assume that this person just sent a template résumé, which means he or she *a)* doesn't really want the job or *b)* doesn't have enough attention to detail to bother customizing his or her objective for my eyes. In either case, I'm not going to bother following up. If the job seeker doesn't care, why should I?

One advantage of including an objective is that it gives *you* clarity about exactly what you're looking for. When I coach students and clients, the first question I always ask is, "What do you want to do?" Everything flows from the answer to that question. Sometimes, we may have to slightly adjust the objective based on the person's level of experience. For example, a culinary student might want to be a sous chef, but probably doesn't have enough experience. In that case, we change the objective to "line cook" because that's what the person is qualified for (once the person is in the job, his or her supervisor will be able to see how good a line cook she is, and will eventually promote her to sous chef).

Your objective is also the foundation of your sound bite. (Refer to Tip 28, "Develop Your Sound Bite, or Elevator Pitch.") To continue with the preceding example, when asked "Who are you?" the culinary student might say, "I'm Bethany, a line cook with five years of kitchen experience and a culinary degree from Le Cordon Bleu, and I hope to be a sous chef one day."

36.
Don't Do It This Way

On the pages that follow is an example of a résumé submitted to me by a student. This is a classic example of "what not to do." Aside from obvious problems, such as spelling, grammatical, and punctuation errors, the information in this résumé is simply not presented in the best possible way.

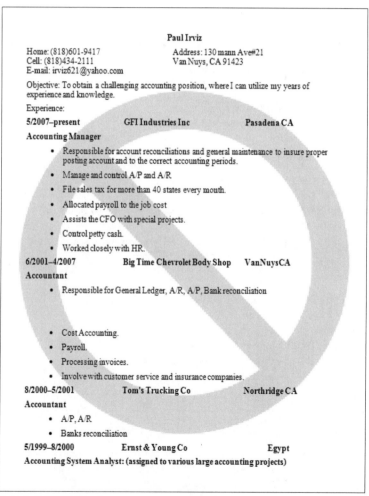

Paul Irviz

Home: (818)601-9417
Cell: (818)434-2111
E-mail: irviz621@yahoo.com

Address: 130 mann Ave#21
Van Nuys, CA 91423

Objective: To obtain a challenging accounting position, where I can utilize my years of experience and knowledge.

Experience:

5/2007–present	GFI Industries Inc	Pasadena CA

Accounting Manager

- Responsible for account reconciliations and general maintenance to insure proper posting account and to the correct accounting periods.
- Manage and control A/P and A/R
- File sales tax for more than 40 states every month.
- Allocated payroll to the job cost
- Assists the CFO with special projects.
- Control petty cash.
- Worked closely with HR.

6/2001–4/2007	Big Time Chevrolet Body Shop	Van Nuys CA

Accountant

- Responsible for General Ledger, A/R, A/P, Bank reconciliation

- Cost Accounting.
- Payroll.
- Processing invoices.
- Involve with customer service and insurance companies.

8/2000–5/2001	Tom's Trucking Co	Northridge CA

Accountant

- A/P, A/R
- Banks reconciliation

5/1999–8/2000	Ernst & Young Co	Egypt

Accounting System Analyst: (assigned to various large accounting projects)

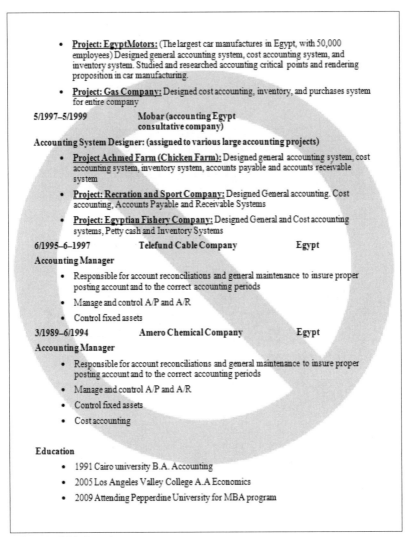

- **Project: EgyptMotors:** (The largest car manufactures in Egypt, with 50,000 employees) Designed general accounting system, cost accounting system, and inventory system. Studied and researched accounting critical points and rendering proposition in car manufacturing.
- **Project: Gas Company:** Designed cost accounting, inventory, and purchases system for entire company

5/1997–5/1999   Mobar (accounting Egypt consultative company)

Accounting System Designer: (assigned to various large accounting projects)

- **Project Achmed Farm (Chicken Farm):** Designed general accounting system, cost accounting system, inventory system, accounts payable and accounts receivable system
- **Project: Recration and Sport Company:** Designed General accounting. Cost accounting, Accounts Payable and Receivable Systems
- **Project: Egyptian Fishery Company:** Designed General and Cost accounting systems, Petty cash and Inventory Systems

6/1995–6–1997   Telefund Cable Company   Egypt

Accounting Manager

- Responsible for account reconciliations and general maintenance to insure proper posting account and to the correct accounting periods
- Manage and control A/P and A/R
- Control fixed assets

3/1989–6/1994   Amero Chemical Company   Egypt

Accounting Manager

- Responsible for account reconciliations and general maintenance to insure proper posting account and to the correct accounting periods
- Manage and control A/P and A/R
- Control fixed assets
- Cost accounting

Education

- 1991 Cairo university B.A. Accounting
- 2005 Los Angeles Valley College A.A Economics
- 2009 Attending Pepperdine University for MBA program

Special Skills

- Over 250 hours of training in accounting system design by Ernst & Young CO
- MAS 90 Accounting Software
- Microsoft Business Navision Software
- QuickBooks Software
- Microsoft Office (Excel, Word, Power Point)

Reference

- Mark Cooper CPA Mobar's CFO (818)421-1210
- David Baum Mobar's HR (719)645-1423
- Harve Big Time Chevrolet Bodyshop Owner (818)475-3621
- Chery Vicko Big Time Chevrolet CFO (818)475-3621
- Harold Garvin CPA Firm Partner (949)412-1128

37.
Do It Like This

The next two pages contain the same résumé, but done correctly. Errors have been fixed, and the information has been reformatted such that it is more appealing to the eye. In addition, the contents of the résumé have been rearranged so the most important items appear first.

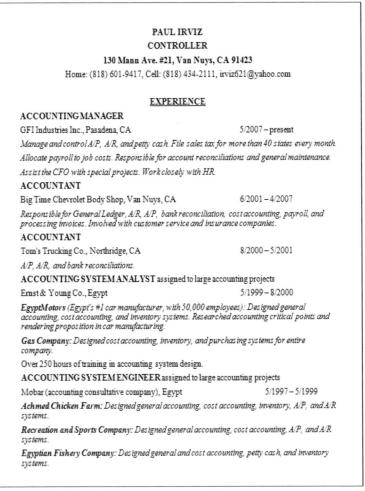

ACCOUNTING MANAGER

Telefund Cable Company, Egypt   6/1995 – 6/1997

Managed and controlled A/P and A/R. Controlled fixed assets. Responsible for account reconciliations and general maintenance.

ACCOUNTING MANAGER

Amero Chemical Company, Egypt   3/1989 – 6/1994

Cost accounting. Managed and controlled A/P and A/R. Controlled fixed assets. Responsible for account reconciliations and general maintenance.

EDUCATION

M.B.A., Pepperdine University	2010
AA in Economics, Los Angeles Valley College	2005
B.A. in Accounting, Cairo University	1991

SOFTWARE

MAS 90 Accounting, Microsoft Business Navision Software, Quick Books Software, Microsoft Office

38.
Why the Changes?

Let's analyze the changes I made to the résumé in Tips 36 and 37—and why I made them.

First: Less is always more in business writing (and speaking). So my first question was, Is it possible to compress this résumé to one page? To reiterate, find out what length résumé the employer prefers. If they don't care, it doesn't matter. But the exercise itself—trying to edit your résumé down to a page or two—will be useful. You'll discover the most important things you've accomplished. Those are the ones you can be confident about delivering to your next employer. In Paul's case, I compressed his contact information to two lines and gave him a brand: Controller. This allowed me to remove his objective.

Now to the question of where to put your education. As with a sound bite, you lead with what's strongest. If you have a lot of experience, put it first. If you don't, begin with your education.

On Paul's résumé, I removed all the bullets and condensed the descriptions for three reasons:

- To save space
- Because English is obviously not Paul's first language
- Because fewer words have more impact

Paul would do well to memorize the key action verbs in his résumé to sell himself in an interview. As we know, employers like action verbs, so give them what they want.

I also eliminated the references, because references do not belong on a résumé. They should be on a separate sheet of paper and presented when the interviewer asks for them. Having this ready will show that you are prepared.

39.

Ask Someone to Proofread Your Résumé

Get someone else to look at your résumé after you finish editing it on your own. A fresh set of eyes can spot redundancies or a lack of clarity in your text and layout. I always have my students and clients do this after they've worked with me.

40.

Update Your Résumé On the Fly

When you've been at a job or on an assignment for a few months and have a good sense of your responsibilities, add your major tasks and accomplishments to your résumé. It's much easier to do it that way than to wait for the job or assignment to be complete. If you pay attention to what you're accomplishing while you're doing it—and write it down at that time—you won't need to try and recall it months or years after the fact. (Plus, you may be pleasantly surprised by how much you actually *have* accomplished!) This practice has the additional benefit of helping you to focus on what matters: producing results. For example, my own résumé says in reference to one position, "Counseled 100+ students in packaging and marketing themselves; achieved over 98% placement rate in summer internships."

41.

Make Sure You're a Good Fit

Before you freshen up your résumé and write your cover letter, read the job description carefully. Are you really a good fit? I have my clients print out the job description and go over it word for word. It's surprising how often people overlook the obvious and see what they want to see, instead of what's actually written.

One client of mine desperately wanted to work for Google, but the job description clearly stated that they needed someone with a lot of technology experience. She, however, had virtually none. It was difficult for her to hear that Google was not likely to consider her, but she finally accepted that she would need to look elsewhere for a company that would embrace the skills she *did* have.

42.

Connect in Your Cover Letter

Your cover letter should consist of three main paragraphs. The first one is what I call "the connection." This is where you need to get the reader's attention. Remember, they're busy. The first thing they want to know is why you're writing to them. What job are you interested in? Are you answering a posting? Where did you find the posting? Were you referred by a mutual contact? If so, mention that contact's name in the first sentence or, if it's an e-mailed cover letter, in the subject line. For example, go with something like, "Dan Jones suggested I contact you."

43.

Show How You're a Match

The second main paragraph in your cover letter is where you show the reader what a great match you are for the position. Go through the job description and highlight the specific requirements they want. Then write about how you match the top three or four. You can even use bullets. For example, you might write:

■ Your job description asks for at least three years of product management experience, and I have five.

■ You require an M.B.A. in finance. I hold an M.B.A. in finance from [name of your university].

■ You need someone who is proficient in both Quicken and QuickBooks. I have taught courses in both programs at my local community college for the past four years.

44.

Make a Plan to Meet

You're not in business until you have a specific date and time in your calendar to talk or meet with the person you've written. Otherwise, it's just bar talk—as in, "Hey, baby, I'll talk to you soon." When exactly is soon? Tomorrow? Next week? Next month? In the third paragraph of your cover letter, add something like, "I look forward to meeting with you in person on Thursday at noon."

The irony in all this is that cover letters are no longer as important as they once were. The percentage of people who now get interviews by sending a résumé and cover letter to a stranger is extremely low. If you've followed my coaching and focused on building relationships, you'll already know the person you're targeting, and a cover letter may not even be necessary!

7

NETWORKING

No great thing is created suddenly.
—Epictetus, Greek Sage and Stoic Philosopher (55–135)

I work with my clients to create and develop their pitch and their narrative—their "story." Then I have them rehearse it until they can comfortably articulate it. Only then do they move to networking. After all, what's the point of networking if, when you meet someone who can potentially be of help to you, you don't know what to say?

I define networking as "making friends for the purpose of advancing your career." Remember: Companies don't hire you; people do. Networking is about connecting with people in a way that brings benefit to both of you. People hire or refer people they know and trust. You need to *develop* new relationships and *deepen* the ones you already have.

Your audience—your market—is potential clients, employers, and people who can refer you. So, with your pitch in place, here's who you target, how you find them, and how to get them interested in who you are and what you have to sell.

45.

Build a Granular Database

The foundation of all your networking efforts will be the creation of a granular database. This is a term I borrowed from digital media, a field in which I worked as a consultant for about nine years. (Note: When you're a freelancer and you have clients—people with whom you work on a contract basis—you call yourself a "consultant.")

Your granular database should be both electronic and portable, residing in whatever device you carry around at all times—your smart phone, iPad, or laptop. You never know when and where you'll need to connect with someone, and you'll want your database accessible.

A traditional contacts database—it was called a "Rolodex" back in the day—contained the names of one's contacts, along with their phone numbers and addresses. A granular database includes these, and so much more:

- Places they've lived.

- Places they've worked, including their job titles.

- Names of their significant others, children, and pets.

- Important dates in their life (birthdays, anniversaries, etc.).

- Their hobbies and interests.

- Their personality traits and quirks, pet peeves, and behaviors—what I call *sweet spots*. These may include tidbits like, "loves Scotch," "very sarcastic," "practical joker," "hates Libertarians," "Anglophile," etc.

You want to begin looking at the people you know as potential sources of work—either direct (they might hire you) or indirect (they could refer you). You are building a detailed profile on everyone you know, beginning with those most likely to hire or refer you.

Why? There's an old saying, "It's not what you know, it's *who* you know." Actually, it's "It's not what you know, it's who you know *and how often you appear on their radar.*" We've established that people in our technology-saturated world are busy. You and your need to find work are not in the forefront of their minds. The granular database is a tool you can update and use for the rest of your working life to keep track of the people you know. It is the foundation for organized and systematic networking. You will eventually have thousands of people with whom you will need to stay in touch, and your granular database is what will allow you to do that.

46.
Meet in Person

So how do you obtain all this detailed personal information? Do you pretend you're a police detective or a reporter and give 'em the third degree? Not at all. What you do is meet with them in person and "break bread." In all cultures, the act of sharing a meal allows people to relax, let their hair down, and begin talking about their personal lives. So that means you need to meet for coffee, breakfast, lunch, or dinner. Choose what they have time for—and what you can afford.

Meeting in person gives you something tweeting, texting, emails, and phone calls don't: time and an environment in which to have a conversation. The personal information shared when you're *schmoozing* (a Yiddish word that means to converse informally) can populate your granular database (see the preceding tip). No Internet superhighway—I don't care how robust and sophisticated it may be—will ever replace the art of the *schmooze*.

You don't want to sit there with a pad and paper taking notes. After all, you're not a detective or a reporter. But when you've said your goodbyes, try to remember all the personal information your companion shared. Write it down, and then enter it in your granular database. Every conversation you have with that person from then on offers an opportunity to fill in the blanks. Over time, you will have a dossier of sorts on everyone in your ever-growing network.

47.

Build a Relationship

Why gather all this information? Obviously, you want to stay in touch with people because they are a source of work. What the granular database allows you to do is to stay in touch with people on a regular basis (you and they will define what's "regular"—and appropriate) for reasons having to do with them (not you).

For example, suppose Ellen owns a company for which you'd like to work. You were introduced by a mutual friend and know her slightly. Ellen is what I like to call "your new best friend." You want to know her better—and to have her know *you* better. You need to find reasons to stay in touch—to stay on her radar. You offer to take her to lunch to get to know each other better and learn ways in which you can help one another. She says she's busy and never takes lunch. So you counteroffer with breakfast—or coffee—and because you have a mutual friend and she doesn't want to be rude, she accepts.

You meet for coffee and begin to get to know each other better. She talks about herself. In addition to learning about her life, you're also looking for what I call "points of resonance"—things you have in common. You may be pleasantly surprised at what or whom you may have in common. This whole campaign of getting to know Ellen—and everyone else you meet—is so that you can turn her from a stranger or someone you know only slightly into a colleague and/or a friend.

Ellen tells you she went to school at Boston College, worked as a broker for Merrill Lynch for three years, has been with her current company for the past eight years, and was appointed vice president a year ago. She broke up with her girlfriend six months ago and isn't dating at the moment. She loves hiking and ballet. In fact, she studied ballet until she was 12 but didn't love it enough to want to become a professional. She has a black cat named Rocco and a mixed breed dog named Duke, and the two of them are best buddies. Duke will be having minor surgery on Monday. Her birthday is coming up in exactly two weeks and she'll be celebrating it at her house on the beach for a week. She hates Facebook, but is a fiend for emailing. And so on. Your coffee with Ellen was not a monologue, but a conversation. She gets to learn about you, too—your background, history, hobbies and goals. And like you, she may well file them away for future reference.

After you and Ellen say your goodbyes, you quickly jot down everything you remember from your conversation. Don't worry if you don't remember everything—you're developing a relationship. You'll have many opportunities to meet again and learn more about her. You can fill in the blanks at a later date.

Later that day, you add Ellen's new information into your smart phone (or tablet or laptop). Then you create alerts about her in your calendar. These might include her birthday (you can learn how old she is at a future meeting), Duke's surgery, and her birthday vacation at the beach. Now you have three reasons to get in touch with her again—and each of them relates to *her* life. The following Tuesday or Wednesday, you send her a short email (that's the best way to reach her, remember?) asking how Duke's surgery went and if he's feeling okay. A few days later, you email Ellen to wish her a happy birthday. She'll appreciate that you remembered. Finally, a few days after she's returned from the beach, you can email her, ask if she had a good time, and tell her that you read that a famous ballet company will be coming to town and if she wants tickets, you know someone at the venue where they'll be performing and can get her a discount.

In other words, you're developing a *relationship* with Ellen—one that may even turn into a friendship. People hire who they know and trust. As you continue to find reasons to stay in touch with Ellen, you'll remain on her radar, and when work becomes available, you're the one she'll think of—and refer.

NOTE *When I've done this sort of thing with the people in my network, the response is invariably, "How thoughtful of you!" I've lost count of how many times a simple courtesy like that has led to work. In truth, I'm not that "thoughtful." I don't clog my brain with details about the lives of the literally thousands of people in my database. I—and you, if you're honest about it—can't even remember all the birthdays and anniversaries of the people in my own family, let alone the name of a professional contact's dog. But my database reminds me of these details.*

Get a meeting and begin to develop a relationship with a friend of a friend or family member. They have the potential of becoming a new colleague. The next part—asking them for and eventually finding work—will present itself later.

Developing relationships is a long-term process. Trust is not built overnight or at one or two meetings. Would you refer someone for a job whom you had just met or hardly knew? Of course not. Think of yourself as a farmer. You plant the seeds—in this case, the seeds of a relationship—nurture them, and they grow over time.

48.

Overcome Your Shyness

If you're saying, "I could never do this. Ellen will know what I'm up to!" or, "I'm too shy. I could never approach someone that way," my answer is one word: *contribution*. By now, you have a good sense of what you offer people in the workplace—and a sound bite that artic-ulates it. Remember: You have something to contribute to Ellen. By giving her a better idea of what you offer, you're doing her—or some-one she knows—a real service. Once she knows what you're about, her response may well be, "Where have you been all my life?" Your shyness deprives her of something of value that she can use.

I'm suggesting you shift your view of networking, perhaps as much as 180 degrees. Networking is about being of service to others and sharing your gifts with them—and you'll ultimately be among the beneficiaries.

49.

Start with Your Family and Friends

You want to start this lifelong networking quest by connecting with anyone and everyone with whom you have something in common. These are the people most likely to help you in your life and career. Human beings are tribal by nature, and people take care of their own.

Begin with your family and friends. Do not assume they know what you've been doing recently or have any idea of what you want to do (or who you might want to meet to get you there). You never know who might know someone in your field until you ask them. This includes the family members who only see you at weddings. Often, these people will tell you, "If there's anything you need, let me know." Well, now you need something! No, it's not a job—not yet, anyway. What you need from those who love you are introductions to people who may be able to help advance your career.

50.

Work Your Affinity Groups

Next, focus on what I call "affinity groups." These might be members of your church; people of your ethnic heritage; your neighbors; fans of your favorite band or sports team; members of your college alumni association, fraternity, or sorority; people who contribute to or volunteer for the same charitable organizations as you; or people with common interests, such as fellow dog owners, golfers, bicyclists, or joggers. What hobbies do you have and what places do you frequent? You have something in common with the people you see there; you're all members of the same club, so to speak.

I was once a guest speaker in a course for graphic artists at Otis College of Art & Design in Los Angeles. The professor, Patty Kovic, had her own graphic design business and was the mother of twin daughters. She told us, "You wouldn't believe how many referrals I've gotten from other people with twins!" The other parents of twins felt a connection—an affinity—with Patty, and were happy to refer work to her.

We all have many groups of people with whom we share something in common. Think about it: You take your dog to a dog park and meet other dog owners, right? You have your dogs in common. If they know what you do for a living, they are apt to refer you because you're "one of them." You ride your bike or jog or play tennis with the same group of people every week. They know you—they're in your affinity group. Use it. These people are happy to help you, but you need to tell them what you do—and what you want.

51.

Enter Through the Side Door

Crafting your résumé into an impeccable representation of who you are professionally is necessary to finding work. But simply sending it out is no longer the most efficient way to accomplish that.

Imagine thousands upon thousands of résumés trying to get through the "front door" of a company. They don't necessarily get read. The front door is a little like a toilet that gets backed up because, well, too much paper has been sent through. I'm not telling you not to send your résumé in response to a posting. What I am saying is that there is a better, more efficient way to find work. And that's through the side door, which I'll label "relationships."

When I was in sales, I had, as one of my bosses described it, "the tenacity of a bulldog on a pant leg." I made 100 phone calls a day—literally—and from that, might get a couple of appointments and one sale. Years later, when I became a Hollywood agent, I learned about access. Access is the ability to make one phone call to a decision-maker, close the sale, and spend the rest of the day at the beach. Smart employers—myself included—are interested in the results, not the process. Neither employers nor clients pat you on the back for the effort you made. It's about efficiency: how little work can you do to produce the desired results? And being able to enter through the side door can save you a *ton* of work.

52.

Take The Meeting—Always

Many people think that social networking is the same as networking. It's a beginning, but nothing will ever replace face-to-face communication. People hire people they know and trust, and trust is developed by getting to know someone in person and over time.

Linda Hudson, the President and CEO of BAE Systems, Inc., said this in an interview in the *New York Times*:

> *Business school graduates come with a great theoretical knowledge about business. But...they have almost no people skills.... We give them all the book smarts, but we don't tend to give them the other skills that go along with business.*

To hone the skills to which Hudson refers, always take the meeting. You never know who can help you in your career. Not every meeting will result in a new client or job, however. Just remember: If you can't make a sale, make a friend. It's a slow seduction; you're getting people to fall in love with you professionally.

53.
Hone Your Stories

As a culture, we've been watching movies for over 100 years because we all love a good story. I have my clients and students practice telling interesting stories about themselves in an engaging way. In the stories you tell, you become the hero of your own life. After all, everyone loves a hero.

For example, I recently worked with a student who had finished a couple of years of college at another school, but hadn't graduated. That could be a red flag to an employer. You never want to volunteer information—either in writing or during an interview—that might make the person doing the hiring nervous. If I had seen this student's résumé before I met him, I might have thought, "Hmm. This guy doesn't finish what he starts." Odds are, employers—who are both busy and deluged with résumés—would have had the same knee-jerk reaction, possibly relegating his résumé to the "round file" (a.k.a. the wastebasket) and disqualifying the candidate. Employers are not inclined to consider that there might be extenuating circumstances; they have so many other résumés and candidates from which to choose.

This student had two options: to omit the time he studied at that school from his résumé or to include it and list some of the courses he *did* complete. The second option—which he chose—meant that in an interview, he would need to be prepared to explain why he didn't graduate from that college. The explanation, or "story," he shared was that he originally thought he wanted to get a business degree but, after a couple of years of coursework, realized that his passion was music. So he put his business studies on hold, planning to complete them at a later date, and enrolled in a music college. This tells an employer that this young man isn't some flaky kid who just does whatever he feels like doing, but a thoughtful young man who is the architect of his career. *That's* the kind of person that people like to work with.

Be prepared to explain or defend everything in your résumé. Employers have every right to ask you about anything they read about you. To prepare for interviews, have a number of friends and/or coaches ask you to tell them two or three stories that explain the choices you have made and to describe the challenges you faced, the things you accomplished, and the experiences you've had in your life.

54.

Think of "Nos" as "Not Yets"

In your quest for work, you'll get a lot of "nos." Don't believe me? Ask any salesperson. When you get a "no"—"No, we're not going to hire you"; "No, we're not going to interview you"; "No, I don't know anyone I can introduce you to"—it's useful to think of it as a "not yet." Remember, a *successful* hitter in baseball fails two-thirds of the time! Or as Margaret Thatcher put it, "You may have to fight a battle more than once to win it." Building a career is a continuous process.

Many years ago, a colleague of mine called me to tell me that he'd been following the arc of my career. (I had made sure to inform him—via email, in this case—every time I published an article, added a client, had a speaking engagement, etc.) Now he was the senior vice president at a startup and wondered if I'd be interested in working for him as a director, earning a high five-figure salary. Politely, I turned him down. (Always be polite and professional; people remember.) I explained that I very much appreciated both the fact that he'd contacted me and the offer (I really did), but that for me to give up my consulting work, I'd need a six-figure salary and a vice presidency. He said no. That "no" didn't mean he didn't like or respect me. It wasn't a reflection of my character, worth, or anything else. My price simply wasn't in his budget—at least, not yet. As it turned out, four months later, he called again and said, "I got you the six figures and want to offer you the job of vice president of business development." I took the job.

The universe does not operate on your timetable. Be patient. Make friends. Plant the seeds. Some of them will grow.

8

TIME MANAGEMENT

I don't need [more] time; I need a deadline.

—Edward Kennedy "Duke" Ellington, Composer,
Pianist, and Bandleader (1899–1974)

Given that these days, everyone's a freelancer—kind of like free agents in professional sports, only not as well paid—it's essential that people treat themselves as a business. Managing money and managing time are the same: You're allocating scarce resources to achieve the desired result in support of that business.

Just as you need to become more conscious and disciplined about money, you need to develop great time-management skills and learn to prioritize your commitments in what's becoming a world in which you are (or will be) busier and busier to focus on the tasks that support your goals. This chapter covers practices you will want to adopt to empower yourself to consistently produce the results you want in your career(s).

55.
Get Your Priorities Straight

Your clients, bosses, employers, and supervisors really don't care how hard or how long you work. They just want to know that you got them what they paid for, on time, and on—or under—budget. That means you must always be as efficient as you possibly can. The less time you spend on a client's project, the higher your hourly rate. If the client pays you $1,000 to get something done, the game for you is how *little* time it will take you. Speaking as a boss, I only care about the results. The members of my team are free to choose the process by which they get their work done, and I highly value efficiency.

When you're managing your time, you need to look at what's important to you and your clients. What's the goal? What are the deliverables? When does the client need them? (If the goal is one you've set for yourself, *you* are the client.) When you begin with the end goal in mind, how you structure your time naturally flows from there.

56.
Set Manageable Milestones

It's helpful to create milestones to give yourself an ongoing sense of accomplishment. Trying to complete a huge project may feel like climbing a gigantic mountain. It can be intimidating. To reduce your stress, picture each phase of the project as a small hill to get over.

For example, my publisher and editor needed this entire book completed by a certain date. Writing a book is a big job. But I broke it down to one chapter at a time, which made it more manageable for me. I "budgeted" my time every day to meet the deadlines we'd set. And with each chapter I completed, I felt more confident that the job would be done according to my client's needs and within the timeframe on which we had all agreed.

57.

Analyze How You Spend Your Time

Try keeping a journal for one week of what you did with your time, in 30-minute increments. Here's an example:

Monday

7:00 a.m.–7:30 a.m. Woke up, stretched
7:30 a.m.–8:00 a.m. Jogged
8:00 a.m.–8:30 a.m. Stretched, showered, dressed
8:30 a.m.–9:00 a.m. Ate breakfast, read the morning paper
9:00 a.m.–9:30 a.m. Checked emails and Facebook
9:30 a.m.–10:00 a.m. Drove to client's office
10:00 a.m.–11:00 a.m. Had meeting with client
11:00 a.m.–12:00 p.m. Had coffee at Starbucks while surfing the Web and playing *Angry Birds*
12:00 p.m.–1:30 p.m. Lunch with a friend
1:30 p.m.–2:00 p.m. Drove to a shopping mall
2:00 p.m.–3:00 p.m. Shopped
3:00 p.m.–3:30 Drove home
3:30 p.m.–4:30 Ate a snack, took a nap
4:30 p.m.–6:00 Created an outline for client's project
…etc.

After a week of journaling, analyze how you spend your time. You're not a machine, so don't expect to use every minute of every day productively. It's okay to take breaks and play *Angry Birds*—or whatever you enjoy doing—to refresh your mind. What you're looking for in your analysis are efficiencies. For example, did you *need* to spend 90 minutes on a shopping trip during a workday? Could the trip have been rescheduled for the weekend—or for that evening, after you'd finished your work? Did you really need a nap in the afternoon? Would another cup of coffee have gotten you back to your work sooner—and maybe helped you to get it done more quickly? Could you have then used the extra time to look for more clients?

I always look to what's going to help me sleep better at night—that's the bottom line on all the choices I make in my life. As tough as it sometimes is to look for work/new clients, being disciplined with your time will make you feel better about yourself. There's nothing like the feeling of having accomplished something to build your confidence.

58.

Do as Little Work as Possible

Believe it or not, that's the goal in the department I supervise. Another way to phrase it is, how efficiently can you produce the results you need? Look at everything in your life—your time, your money, the environment in which you work, your body (the environment you inhabit). Are they aligned with your commitment to produce the best work you can, at all times?

All of the above are interrelated. Ask yourself: Am I getting enough sleep? Am I getting up early enough to handle the things I need to do to prepare for my day? These might include eating well, meditating, yoga, spending time with your family, reading and researching, having a healthy meal, etc. The things you have to do to honor your commitments might begin to feel less like chores if you approach them in the spirit of doing them to help yourself be more prepared. As J.M. Barrie, the author of *Peter Pan*, said, "Nothing is really work unless you would rather be doing something else."

The same cost/benefit ratio that you use for money can also be used to judge what you're doing with your time. Playing *Angry Birds* is fun—but at what point does it begin to take away time from the project you've contracted to complete? Managing time means just that: You get to decide when it's time to play and when it's time to get back to work. Here's a time-management mantra that I've used for many years: "Does it cost me money or does it make me money?" Every choice I make in business is based on that phrase.

I recently taught a class during which the subject of procrastination came up. "Show of hands," I asked, "how many of you have a problem with procrastinating?" Every hand shot up. It's my belief that if you have a goal and you want to achieve it badly enough, procrastination ceases to be an issue. We procrastinate about the things we don't want to do. If you have an issue with procrastination, maybe the problem isn't you—maybe you're just not doing something you want to do.

9

ORGANIZATION
(YOURS AND THEIRS)

I don't want to know what the law is, I want to know who the judge is. .
—Roy Cohn, Attorney, Chief Counsel to Senator Joseph McCarthy
(1927–1986)

Finding work is a never-ending campaign. Like a military campaign, you need to be armed before you go into battle (and looking for work can sometimes feel like just that: a battle). This chapter outlines—to continue the metaphor—how you navigate the battle-field, as well as the artillery you'll need. (Fortunately, in this war, no one gets maimed, killed, or taken prisoner!)

59.

Identify an Organization's Formal Structure

The formal structure of an organization deals with the relationships between authority figures and subordinates. It's often outlined in an organizational chart ("org chart" for short), which illustrates who's in charge and who reports to whom. This chart is hierarchical and includes job titles and clear lines of authority. It's the "official version."

If you're looking for a job in the traditional manner, your résumé and cover letter will, hopefully, journey through the hierarchy described in an org chart. Its first stop will be a subordinate in the human resources department ("the place where résumés go to die"). Then, if you're lucky, it *may* go to a subordinate in the department where you want to work. Next, after a successful interview, it *might* proceed to a mid-level person in that same department for a follow-up interview. It's usually a long and slow process, like a paper salmon swimming upstream. And all too often, your résumé—and your chances—die along the way. Why? Maybe because the company hired someone internally. Or maybe the CEO's niece just graduated from college and needed a job. (Don't ever discount nepotism.) Whatever the reason, your chances of getting work using this route—the formal route—are not good.

If you talk to people who've been in the working world for any appreciable length of time, 95% of them will tell you, "I got my job because I knew someone." I want *you* to be one of the people who "knew someone" so you'll be the one who gets the job. The way to do that is often by avoiding the formal structure in the organization for which you want to work altogether or by opening a second front.

60.

Identify an Organization's Informal Structure

The informal structure of any organization is usually how things *really* work. It's based on relationships and connections—doing favors for and taking care of the people who have your back. If you work inside an organization, no doubt there are the official, proscribed means of communication (forms, requests, procedures, etc.). But if you *really* need to get something done, it's your relationships with co-workers that grease the wheels and produce the results. The personal connections you've formed with people are what cut through the red tape and speed the process, saving both time and energy.

How this relates to finding work is that while you may be looking for work via traditional means (answering job postings, filling out online forms, and sending in your résumé, cover letter, letters of reference, transcripts, and other supporting documents), you're simultaneously chasing the people you know in the company—and the people you know who know people who work there—to get you in the door.

When Robert F. Kennedy was the campaign manager for his brother, John F. Kennedy, during his run for the presidency in 1960, he described his campaign strategy as, "on all fronts at all times." I never tell a client or a student *not* to pursue the traditional route—you still can find work that way. But it's no longer the most efficient means of doing so. So you try both. Most likely, however, you'll find that the "new" way—via the organization's informal structure, or your network of relationships—will be your best bet.

61.

Make Friends with the Gatekeepers

"Gatekeepers" are those people who are sometimes derisively called "the little people"—the security guards, janitors, secretaries, and assistants in any organization. It's critical that you treat these people with the utmost respect. I hold a doctorate in organizational leadership, and my studies with and experience in organizations have shown me that it's essential to treat *everyone* in an organization well, because everyone matters.

Suppose you've developed a business relationship with a vice president at POP industries. I'll call her Julie. Because you're a snob, you've always been dismissive of Julie's assistant, Matt, when you've spoken to him on the phone or visited Julie at the office. After all, he's just an underling! Besides, you don't think Matt notices.

Wrong. Matt *does* notice.

One day, you hear about a job in Julie's department. You *know* the job is meant for you—but you must get in to see her that morning. So you call, and you reach Matt. And Matt—whose entire sphere of power involves granting or denying people access to Julie, and who has been dying to pay you back for all the insults and slights he's received from you for the past year—says that Julie is in an important meeting and can't be disturbed. So she never learns that you're interested in the job, and it goes to someone else.

Be kind and respectful to *everyone* you work with—or will work with some day. Not only is it the decent thing to do, it makes good business sense.

62.
Follow Up!

Nothing indicates professionalism, separating the men from the boys and the women from the girls, as much your ability to follow up—to keep your word and do what you said you'd do. After all, who you are, what defines your reputation, is that people can count on you, consistently. Once, when a potential client asked a colleague of mine who I was, she replied, "When you want something from Chaz, you get it." It was one of the finest compliments I've ever received. Isn't that how *you'd* like to be known—as someone who always delivers?

This kind of behavior is something you can build into your granular database. (You learned about granular databases in Chapter 7, "Networking.") If you tell a colleague you will call him on Tuesday at 10:00 a.m., you should enter that into your granular database—and CALL HIM ON TUESDAY AT 10:00 A.M.! You'd be surprised how this simple practice will separate you from the pack.

For some reason, many (most?) people are unreliable. You just can't count on them. I've heard a million of excuses from students about why they didn't turn in an assignment on time. "I forgot my flash drive." "My car broke down." "I brought the wrong backpack." "My printer wasn't working this morning." "My hard drive got corrupted." And so on, and so forth. As a professor, *I don't care*. And if I were someone's supervisor at work, and that person came up with a lame excuse as to why he didn't deliver what he promised, *I would care even less*. Likewise, your clients and the people with whom you seek to work aren't interested in excuses when you don't do what you say you're going to do.

I recently set up an important meeting with a department chair for a student who needed some coaching. Incredibly, the student failed to show up for the meeting. I asked my staff about it, and they told me the student was "a bit of a flake." The next time I saw the student, I confronted her, asking if she had put the meeting in the calendar in her phone. She said she had, but that she often forgets to check it. I said that was unacceptable. She needed to set up a system for herself so she would never forget to check her calendar again—whether it was an alert on her phone, a stickie on her mirror, or a daily call from a friend.

Because she was a student, I was somewhat forgiving. But if *you* do that sort of thing to a client (or potential client), be prepared for them to stop working with you. If you're notoriously sloppy about following up, create a system that forces you to remember to do what you said you'd do. Be like a friend of mine, who often had trouble getting up in the morning. When he landed a new job that really mattered to him, he bought four alarm clocks to wake him every morning. He was never late for work again.

63.

Get Organized for Networking

You may not love the analogy, but think of the marketing materials you use to promote yourself as guns in your holster. Have them with you whenever you might need them—and pull them out as appropriate. These materials include the following:

- **Business cards.** These should be easy to read, and should contain appropriate information such as your name, phone number(s), email address, website, street address, and a slug line ("Editor," "Graphic Design," "IT Consulting," etc.). Check with the people in your industry to learn what fits. A business card with an artistic pattern on colored cardstock would probably be inappropriate for an accountant, but just right for a video editor.

- **Your online presence.** If people in your industry expect you to have an online presence, you must give it to them. Learn where you should be. LinkedIn? Facebook? Twitter? Your own website? Videos of your work on YouTube? Should you carry around an iPad or a laptop so you can easily demo your work to the people you meet?

In addition, if you'll be attending networking events—such as conferences, conventions, or trade shows—carry pens, paper, and breath mints with you. Also bring product samples, a bio or résumé, your portfolio on a flash drive, bottled water, a bag in which to carry the stuff you pick up, etc. (The list will vary according to the field you work in and the type of event it is.) Finally, wear attire appropriate to your industry and the event.

One word of caution about these events (as well as career fairs): Lower your expectations. The people you'll be meeting have priorities other than hiring you. Many are there to sell their wares, or are attending as buyers. Don't go with the intention of finding work, expecting to hand out résumés and get on-site interviews. Otherwise, you will probably be very disappointed. Instead, go with the intention of meeting people and learning about new products and trends in your industry. Have fun, make friends, and pick up information and business cards—and then follow up afterward.

10

GETTING OUT OF
YOUR OWN WAY

This is the true joy in life, the being used for a purpose recognized by yourself as a mighty one; the being a force of nature instead of a feverish, selfish little clod of ailments and grievances complaining that the world will not devote itself to making you happy. I am of the opinion that my life belongs to the whole community, and as long as I live it is my privilege to do for it whatever I can. I want to be thoroughly used up when I die, for the harder I work the more I live. I rejoice in life for its own sake. Life is no "brief candle" for me. It is a sort of splendid torch which I have got hold of for the moment, and I want to make it burn as brightly as possible before handing it on to future generations.

—George Bernard Shaw, Playwright, Essayist, Novelist,
and Short Story Writer (1856–1950)

Despite all the useful coaching you may absorb from this book and the practices you may now be following, you may not be getting the results you want. There may be a number of explanations:

- You haven't been following the practices long enough. If you're a farmer, it's not enough to plant seeds, water them, and give them sufficient sunlight; you also need to be patient. Sure, you could always stand over them and scream, "GROW!" But that's only going to make you hoarse and/or angry—while making absolutely no difference whatsoever to the seeds.

- You need to adjust your processes. What's effective? What's *not* working? What are you doing too much—or too little? What do you need to change in your marketing efforts? Talk to your colleagues and mentors, get advice, and do some tweaking.

- Sometimes you may do all the right things and not get the results you were after. Life offers no guarantees. Sorry.

- You have issues—emotional or otherwise—that are in the way.

This chapter will deal with the fourth explanation.

64.

Get Coaching

There will be times when you're unsure about your career direction or your career choices, or you just need a reality check on what you're doing with your life. That's a good time to sit down with your friends and get some coaching. Find a comfortable, quiet place and ask them to tell you how they see you professionally. What are your strengths? When they think of you or talk to other people about you, what words come to mind? Conversely, what are you *not* good at?

Remember, these are your friends. They love you. They're the ones who will always give you an honest assessment, who'll be there to tell you what you *need* to hear—even if it isn't what you may *want* to hear. Your job is to listen and be open-minded. These people love you holistically—for the good person you are, despite any silly or irritating habits you may have. If you approach this process with humility and as a learning experience, you may be very pleasantly surprised by what you will learn. Your friends *know* you. Take their advice seriously, and then follow it.

I began my teaching career many years ago at UCLA Extension. Before then, I had never thought much about teaching, but I quickly found that I loved it. I continued teaching there once a year, but never considered education as a career option. I was working in digital media, and teaching was just something I did on the side, for fun. Then, in 2000, the dot-com bubble burst. My consulting work in digital media dried up. A friend who had known me for awhile and seen me teach suggested I look into being a college professor as a full-time career. My first impulse was to say no, but she finally convinced me—or maybe I slowly realized—that teaching was a viable career option, and I began pursuing it. In a sense, she understood me better than I did. And *I* was smart enough to surrender to her better perspective and prescient advice.

I'm still a college professor. I have what I wish for you—work I love that I'd do for free, but that I do so well that people pay me a lot of money for it.

65.

Deal with Your Fear of Success

Everyone knows about fear of failure. It's often what keeps people from taking risks, trying new things, and stepping out into the unknown. But there's another fear: fear of success. With fear of success, it's actually easier and safer to *not* take risks, try new things, or step out into the unknown because the alternative is far scarier.

If you try to do something and *succeed*, it puts you into a whole new realm. You're no longer in the safe space you've always been—the familiar place where your friends can commiserate with you, filled with the ongoing drama called some variation of "Poor Me I've Tried So Hard But Life Is Tough And No One Really Cares."

But if you *succeed*—if you actually accomplish what you said you would—you put yourself in a more challenging situation. *You actually have to produce results*. You have to *deliver* on the things you promised to do for others. Can you do it? What if they find out you're really a fraud? Better to *not* try and just go with what you know. That's less scary.

Does this sound like you? If the answer is yes, you'll want to notice this type of behavior, acknowledge it, and push through it. It's part of the human condition to feel you're a fraud and that others will "find you out." You're not alone. Do it *anyway*. People need the gifts you offer. Don't deny them that privilege.

66.

Conquer Shyness

In a world in which everyone is always hustling for work, you can't afford to be shy or modest. You may be saying, "I could *never* talk myself up/sell myself/approach strangers in that way" (or some variation of that internal conversation). Maybe it feels like bragging. But I'm here to tell you, you're wrong.

Some people are genuinely shy—something that's painfully difficult to overcome. You may *never* enjoy talking to people about yourself. But you need to learn how to do it. Having that ability will lead to work for you—work that you love and are meant to do. You have my permission to go to networking events, smile, talk to strangers, and pitch yourself—and get sick to your stomach afterward. What matters is that *you did what you needed to do.* Congratulations!

Here are some suggestions to help make this process less painful:

- **Join Toastmasters International.** This nonprofit educational organization operates clubs worldwide to help members improve their communication, public-speaking, and leadership skills. Attend a meeting—or lots of meetings. The first thing you'll notice is that you're not alone—one of the many benefits of *any* networking you do. Many people have difficulty communicating with strangers and/or speaking in public. Toastmasters is a supportive environment that will help you manage these fears while increasing your confidence.

- **Take acting classes.** Taking acting classes is a wonderful way to get you out of your head. Plus, there's the possibility that performing in front of people could actually be *fun*. You may be saying, "Acting means being someone else. When I have to network for business, I can't hide behind a character; I have to be *me*." Let me clue you in: *Everything* is a performance. People are *always* "on." Whenever you're selling yourself, you need to appear upbeat, positive, and happy—*whether you feel like it or not*. It's all acting. So learn from the masters how it's done. You might also discover how joyful an experience acting can be!

- **Do therapy.** Sometimes, the fears you have are deep-seated. They may even extend back to your childhood. That's nothing to be ashamed of. In fact, you deserve to be congratulated for pushing yourself hard enough in your job search to discover fears that may have been getting in your way your whole life. Now it's time to continue by finding professional help so you can understand what caused the fear and take the appropriate steps to manage it.

67.

Learn to Read Body Language

You may be shocked to learn that people in the business world sometimes lie. (Okay, maybe that's not so shocking.) If you want to discover what people are *truly* communicating, stop paying so much attention to what they say in words and begin focusing on their body language. Bodies—that includes eyes, hands, and facial expressions—are where the truth resides. You can find many videos about nonverbal communication on YouTube that demonstrate how to detect the *real* message a person is sending.

In job interviews, I don't pay much attention to the words being spoken by the candidate. Instead, I focus on what their bodies are telegraphing. It gives me a much more accurate read on who a candidate is—and if I'm interested in having that person join my team. I also use this ability in a classroom setting to gauge whether my students are getting bored. If so, I might need to move on to another exercise or maybe just give them a short break. I even employ it in meetings so I can tell if I'm getting my point across or how others are responding to what's being discussed. Are they upset? Confused? Distracted? Happy?

Being able to read body language is one of my most valuable skills. It allows me to monitor and, if need be, quickly adjust my style of communication—my tone, volume, speed of delivery, body posture, hand gestures, etc.—in response to whomever I'm talking to. This has made me a far more effective communicator. After all, if no one's paying attention to me or getting what I'm saying, why bother to continue talking? The point of communication is not to impress the listener with your public speaking prowess or large vocabulary, but to have an impact on him or her.

I "read" my staff. From the moment they walk in the office in the morning, I have a sense of how they are feeling, before they say a word. I can tell by how they carry themselves whether they're ill or upset. If I perceive that they are, I always ask them if something's wrong. Often, it's just something small—maybe they were stuck in traffic on the way to the office. Regardless, at that point, I just need to let them vent for a few moments to release their frustration so they can be fully present for the day's work ahead. As someone said, "A coach [or in this case, a boss] is only as good as his team feels."

68.
Create Your Look

I sometimes wear a skull cap at work. It has no religious significance—although at times I've been asked if I'm a Muslim or an Orthodox Jew. I wear it because it protects my head from the sun and keeps my head warm when it's cold. It's also unusual and somewhat distinctive. It's become my "look." There are students on campus who don't remember Dr. Chaz—until someone reminds them what I look like. Then I become "the dude with the cap." I don't mind. The cap makes me memorable.

You want to be memorable to the people in *your* industry. We are a visually oriented society. People remember what they see. Is there something you can do to create a look for yourself that people will recall? Maybe you could be "the fellow who wears those great ties." Or, "the woman with the colorful scarves." Or, "the guy with those great eyeglass frames." Be a *character*—someone with a distinctive look. You don't want to be pigeonholed, but isn't it better to be remembered for *something* rather than not at all? Think of it this way: If you're acting, you might as well be in costume.

Your look will go hand in hand with an impeccable presentation—nails, teeth, hair, shined shoes, clean and well-pressed clothes, etc. And of course, it needs to be appropriate to your industry. You belong, and are distinctive. For example, a soul patch in financial services might denote you as "not one of us," whereas it would be completely appropriate in a music publishing company. Your visual presentation is like playing dress-up. Have fun with it!

11

Building a Name
for Yourself
in Your Field

A good reputation is more valuable than money.
　　　　　—Publilius Syrus, Latin Writer of Maxims (1st century B.C.E.)

S o now you're out there, attending events, networking, meeting
people and getting to know them. But you're still just another
face. What can you do so people know *you*? What will distinguish you? This chapter talks about the things you can do to build your
brand and pull ahead of the pack.

69.

Become an Expert

Why should people pay special attention to *you*? Perhaps the better question to ask is, what can you do for *them*? What do they need that you can provide?

One thing people need is information—useful intelligence they can apply to their working lives and businesses. Perhaps you're becoming involved in a different field—something that allows you a fresh perspective. You can see the practices and trends through new, unjaded eyes. People in any field crave a new way to look at things, a different angle that might offer insight into the future. The person who offers that could be you.

Choose a particular niche in your field that's been underexplored or neglected altogether—some growth area that people haven't been paying attention to. I did this in higher education. I saw an area in my field—career development—that had been unmined. Career development (a.k.a. career counseling, or career services) had been a staple of higher education for decades. Indeed, there had long been a career department in every college and university in the country. No doubt, most people just figured there wasn't much more to say about it. It worked, and everyone knew what it did. There was nothing worth changing or fixing. To most people, it was like the student union found in virtually all universities—it was just *there*.

Au contraire, mon ami. I quickly discovered that there was *a lot* wrong with how career services were delivered in higher education.

In fact, the way I saw it, career services departments simply weren't delivering. There was a disconnect between academia, which focused far too much on outdated theory and rote learning, and the business world, which prized practical skills and the ability to think critically, solve problems, and communicate. I also saw that whatever efforts career services *did* make were insufficient, outmoded, or both. Career services offered one-on-one counseling, but the subject matter was limited to résumés. It should also have included branding, networking, and mock interviews. Moreover, if career courses were available, they were usually offered as an elective during senior year—too little and too late.

As someone who came to higher education from the business world, I had a different take on the subject. But why would anyone listen to *me*? I knew I had something unique to contribute, but I had to build credibility first. I needed to become an expert, somewhat of an authority in the field.

How did I get from being an unknown to here, a doctor and the author of a book on the subject, published by one of the largest publishers in the world? Like any campaign, one carefully plotted step at a time. And you can become an expert in your field, too.

First, look at what you can offer. Can you write? Are you good at public speaking? Can you produce meetings? Do you have a talent for connecting people? I am a good coach, so I began by contacting people. I located someone I'd known years before who was now running a school. We had a long lunch during which we caught up and I got to pitch him on the new skills I'd learned and what I thought I could do for him. He invited me to talk to his students about how to pitch themselves. I'd been in sales (video retailing and video post production) and had been an agent for a large theatrical agency. By that time, I had also done some teaching. We agreed that my combination of skills and experiences made me a good candidate to guest-lecture at his school on a regular basis.

You want to look at your strengths and see how you can leverage them into the next opportunity in your life. For me, it was this:

Teaching + Selling = Teaching Students How to Sell Themselves.

70.

Present

Associations in every field hold conferences and conventions. And at every conference and convention, there are presentations and panels. And the people who book those presentations and panels need speakers. Preferably, those speakers are experts, but if not, then they're people who at least work in the field, know something about it, and might be entertaining—or at least lively—so the audience won't get bored. If you've followed my advice, you're a member of the associations in your field that produce these events. So volunteer with those associations to serve as a presenter or panelist for its next conference or convention.

If you're not quite an expert (yet), begin by offering to *moderate* a panel. Convince them that you can ask good questions and keep things upbeat and interesting. Being a moderator is a good place to start building your brand among your colleagues. The networking opportunities are outstanding. The fact that you're the moderator signals to panelists (some of whom will actually be respected experts in your field) that you're a colleague worthy of their time and respect. Eventually, you'll build up enough credibility to be a panelist, and later you'll be invited to be a presenter.

71.
Publish

People in your field need to know how you think, and to be able to share what you have to say with others. But who's going to publish content from an unknown? Well, *you* are. Start a blog (Wordpress and Tumblr are two of the best resources for bloggers) and let your colleagues know where they can locate your brilliant opinions. Better yet, have them sign up to receive your blog posts on a regular basis. The power and ease of social networking will allow your "fan base" to spread the word that you are someone who's worth paying attention to. If you're not a good writer, find an editor who can translate your thoughts into good copy.

The next step in your quest to be "an authority in your field whose opinions people read" is to publish in someone else's publication. The publishing landscape has changed enormously in the past few years. When I began working in digital media in the early 1990s, we said that the Internet would change everything. It has. In publishing, that means it's probably not a good idea to expect to be paid to write. Consider it a loss leader—an investment that can create revenue-producing opportunities (consulting, a job, etc.).

You can begin by being an interviewee or a writer for a friend or colleague's blog. That can move you to being quoted as an expert by a well-known industry publication. The final step is to write a book. Trust me, nothing creates credibility like being a published author. Be aware, however, that you will probably have to self-publish. If you're Stephen King or James Patterson, then the big publishing houses will be happy to work with you. Your celebrity includes a built-in fan base. If you're not a "name," however, then you self-publish. Think of it as another investment in your career. Being an author, you'll be treated with a greater degree of respect. That's been true for me. In my field, however, title *really* matters. So I decided to get my doctorate before my first book was published so the cover would read "*Dr.* Austin." You'll need to decide what's going to work in your industry.

I'll add a caveat to this tip: If you don't write well and can't find an editor, don't go this route. There are other ways to become an expert in your industry if writing is not one of your strengths. For example, if you're opinionated and well-spoken, you can be someone other writers contact for a pithy quote on a regular basis. It'll be your words—but someone else will have done the writing for you.

72.

Create Your Very Own Dog and Pony Show

As you explore your niche, you'll want to create a presentation that explains your point of view—your very own dog and pony show. For me, it was—and is—that the way in which career training is delivered in higher education needs to be revolutionized. I am an evangelist for this, and I've traveled all over the country spreading the word. What issue have you found in *your* field that needs to be addressed, changed, or overhauled? What do you believe in so much that you are willing to talk to anyone who will listen?

As you know, we're a visually oriented society, so your dog and pony show will probably need to include some sort of PowerPoint presentation. I have a lot of experience with PowerPoint, so here's a bit of advice: Your presentation needs to be clean (not cluttered) with interesting visuals and a *minimal* amount of text that's large and easy to read. Begin with the story. What's your narrative? Consider your visual presentation as a series of headlines that complement what you're saying.

I've shown some version of my PowerPoint presentation probably 400 times to audiences ranging from a single student, client, or colleague to hundreds of people in an auditorium. I never get tired of it in part because I update it on a regular basis, but mainly because I truly believe that what I'm talking about has value to my viewers and listeners and that they need—and deserve—to hear it. The same goes for you. Your ideas will help you move your industry forward. They're also what will help you build a name for yourself and be perceived as an expert in your field.

73.

Be the Connector

When I worked in the digital media industry, especially when I was the vice president of the International Interactive Communications Society (IICS), then the leading association in digital media, I made it my business to build a robust database of contacts. My prowess was not on the technical side; it was in connecting people. It got to the point where people would say, "Chaz knows everybody." I didn't, of course, but that was the perception.

The more you build your database, the more details you know about the people who inhabit it, the greater the chances of you connecting them with each other. And the more connections you make, the greater your value. You become a resource, a "go-to" person. You may not know everyone, but you can be one person away from everyone or everything your contacts may need.

Suppose a contact—let's call her Laura—needs a horse trainer. You don't own a horse. In fact, you're not much of a rider yourself. So you do a search in your database for "horses," and your friend Ann's name appears. You call her, and sure enough, she knows a good horse trainer. So you put Laura and Ann in touch. Ann refers her horse's trainer to Laura. Laura is happy. Ann is happy to have referred her trainer. Both of them are happy with you for having connected them. Even better, without having it spelled out to them, Laura and Ann owe you—and they know it. Their payback may be indirect, but someday, they will probably return the favor in some way.

Business is trading favors. A colleague of mine lives by the maxim, "I want all my friends working. That way, they're all in a position to help me." You want to be the nexus for as many people as you can, the "fixer," the person who has done enough favors for enough people that when someone needs something done—from a reservation at an exclusive restaurant to access to an important executive—you're the person they call on, because *you're* the one who can get things done. In the Yiddish language, you're a *macher* (the "ch" is pronounced the same as the "ch" in Johann Sebastian Bach), a mover, a person of influence.

Many or even most of the favors you'll do will be at no charge. Don't be afraid to donate your time to others, especially when you're beginning to navigate an industry. No one says no to free labor, and helping out in this way is an easy way to ingratiate yourself. Be gracious about it. Be aware, however, that giving it away has a limited shelf life. After awhile, you'll have built enough of a name for yourself that you won't have the time to donate your services. Besides, no one would dare ask a respected authority to do that!

12

CONTINUING TO LEARN AND IMPROVE

Education is never completed until you die.
—Robert E. Lee, Commander of the Confederate Army
of Northern Virginia (1807–1870)

S tudies show that more than 40% of college graduates will never read another book after they graduate. That's one of the saddest statistics I've ever read. How is it that our educational system failed students to such an extent that reading is not seen as a joyous discovery, but a chore that students can cease to perform after they've earned a degree? I've actually taught college students who believed they'd be finished with learning after they graduated!

I'm not talking about *you*, of course. (At least, I hope not!) No, you're someone who is passionate about the field in which you work (or plan to work), and you read everything you can because you love learning. This chapter will help you focus on what you need to read and learn to keep you current and informed—and employable.

74.

Give 'Em What They Want

In every field, certain things are required before you can "get in the door." In the financial sector, that might be an MBA. In counseling, it might be an MSW or an MFT. In my field, education, if you want to teach at the college level, you must have a master's degree. If you're shooting for a tenured professorship, a doctorate is required.

You might be saying, "This isn't fair. I have years of real-world experience that's far more practical than any silly degree." Well, good for you. But them's the rules. Sorry. A degree won't necessarily make you that much smarter or better at what you do, but if the people doing the hiring want you to have one, then it's up to you to go get it. Think of it as a rite of passage, the accomplishment that will get you to the next level, the new starting line.

I regularly counsel my students and clients about the value of obtaining more education and/or additional degrees. If it makes sense for them to do that—and it varies from person to person—I always caution them to lower their expectations before they begin their educational journey. What they'll be learning should not be their main focus. In terms of priorities, first on their list will be the credibility they'll enjoy from having attained that degree and the doors it will open. Second is the people they'll meet and how they'll be able to leverage those relationships in the future to further their careers. In third place is what they might learn.

Unfortunately, higher education—even at its highest levels—is still full of theory and busy work, and not much that's practical and applicable. Generally, professors still teach the way they've taught for the past 100 years: by having students memorize factoids and spit them back out on a test. I speak both as a student who's suffered during the majority of my 20 years of schooling and three degrees and as an educator who sees the futility of continuing to try to engage students in a so-called "learning process" that long ago proved bankrupt.

Generally, the more degrees you have, the better, because more degrees equals more options. Of course, you will have to weigh their value against the debt you may have to incur to obtain them. If you're going to pursue another degree, learn whatever you can when you're back in school. Just don't expect much.

75.

Learn a New Language

One of the things that distinguishes one field of endeavor from another is the language that's spoken there. Just as you need to speak the language if you move to a foreign country, you must learn to speak an industry's native tongue if you want to be part of it. That's how your colleagues will know you're "one of them."

Each field has its own buzzwords, acronyms, and vernacular expressions. Here are a few: rubric, WASC, gainful employment stats, ABD, MOOCs, pedagogy. All these are terms endemic to higher education, where *I* live. If you don't work in higher education, I wouldn't expect you to know what they mean—or care. But working in higher ed requires that I both understand and know how to use these terms.

76.

Be Proficient with the Latest...

...everything! Our world is moving online, and nothing says "old fogey" like someone who hasn't kept up with the latest trends in mobile, social media, etc. *Every* field and business is being affected by this migration. If you're fighting Facebook or dismissing Twitter, cut it out. Companies are hiring social media experts and directors of data analytics—titles that didn't even *exist* a few years ago. You can't afford to be left behind!

As part of your research into moving up in your own field or finding your place in a new one, find out what software and apps people in that field are using and how to use them. You need to be proficient in them so you don't become redundant.

It's not hard to discover what you'll need to learn. Could the problem be—especially if you're past a certain age—that you're *resisting*? Remember: There will *never* be a time in your career when you can stop learning. So you might as well dive in, immerse yourself in what's new, and maybe—dare I say it?—*embrace* it. No, Facebook is not just for kids. In fact, 46% of people who are online use social networking sites. By 46%, I mean 46% of people who are *65 and older*. I'm sorry, what was your excuse again?

What you'll discover is that sites and apps like Facebook, Twitter, Pinterest, and Instagram have become far more than ways for young people to waste time with their friends; these days, they're new and highly effective marketing platforms for business. Facebook has well over a billion users worldwide. My attitude about social phenomena is that if a lot of people are using it—and "over a billion" certainly qualifies as "a lot"—or it's being used/listened to/watched after many years (laptops, Beethoven, *Star Wars*), then you need to pay attention to it. In other words, something's going on there, and you need to know why people respond to it, why it resonates for them, and what they're getting from it. If people keep coming back for more, there's something there that they need. You don't have to *like* Facebook (or Beethoven), but it makes sense to learn to appreciate it. And if it can be helpful in furthering your career, you need to learn how to *use* it.

77.

Stay on Top of Things

As you research and study to grow in your field, there are a number of areas you'll want to pursue:

- What are the most popular software programs? Be thoroughly proficient with *all* of them—beginning with MS Office (if you don't already know it). Look at what computer proficiencies companies need—and are paying for. Database programs? (If so, which ones?) Adobe Creative Suite? Skype? Photoshop? Google Apps? What do you know about cloud computing?

- What online publications/newsfeeds/alerts do you get and *read regularly?* Our world is changing constantly and instantaneously. Are you on top of things? Even better, can you spot where things are headed?

- Are you still reading *offline* publications? Books? Business magazines, newspapers, or trade journals? Yes, I know most of them have online editions. (I subscribe to and read *The New York Times*, *The New Yorker*, and *The Atlantic Monthly* online.) And yes, I know companies use algorithms to feed you content they think you'll want to read. But what about the serendipity factor—i.e., when you're leafing through the print edition of a daily paper or a magazine and you find something of interest that you never would have looked for and maybe never even have *thought* about before, but is fascinating and maybe useful in your work and life? Make room for the unexpected.

78.

Go Back to Campus

Whether you're returning to school to earn another degree or not, your college campus—and library (virtual or actual)—is always a place of learning. Don't discount the value of mining its resources and staying in touch with the people who work there. Colleges and universities are mandated to explore what is new in the world. Your job is to learn what's new in your field. See the connection? Ask for guidance from the school's librarians. I've found them to be enormously useful in helping me find what I'm looking for—and what I *wasn't* looking for but very much need to know.

But there's more you can do at your school. Look at you alma mater as a place to network. Someone once said that home is the place where they have to take you in. The same goes for your school. You'll always be an alum, and where you went to school will always be your "home." Get active in your alumni association. This is an affinity group—they *have* to talk to you. It's a perfect place to meet staff, faculty, and other alumni who may well be on the cutting edge of discoveries in the very field you're in or getting into. Apart from any learning you might do, who knows what relationships you may forge—relationships that could lead to all kinds of opportunities? Network all over campus, volunteer to participate in events, and join committees. Volunteering will raise your profile—and can sometimes lead to paid work. *Boola boola*!

13

STAYING SANE

You can't get much done in life if you only work on the days when you feel good.

—Jerry West, Professional Basketball Player
and Basketball Executive (1938–)

W hen undertaking big challenges—such as finding work—it's always useful to consider a worst-case scenario. Finding work can be a long, arduous, frustrating, and occasionally scary process—*but you're not going to die*. Eventually, you *will* find work. "Eventually" may mean a few weeks or a few months, but there will be an end to your search. This chapter offers ideas and practices to help you stay positive and upbeat—especially at those times when you may feel like there's no hope.

79.

Get Out of Your Head

Thinking is overrated. That may seem like an odd idea coming from someone who holds a doctorate, but we human beings do have a tendency to overthink things—particularly when we're alone. It's as if you have a tape in your head that keeps looping back, repeating the same conversation over and over again.

What's happening is that your fear and anxiety are becoming amplified. Ever notice how the conversation on that tape is usually a negative one? It never seems to be about how wonderful you are. Its subject matter is invariably about something you're lacking. When you're looking for work, your mind is probably telling you things like, "You're not good enough," "You're too old," "You're too young," "You don't have enough education," "You're overqualified," "You're underqualified," "No one cares," "The job market is tough," "You shouldn't have left that last job," "What about the gap in your résumé," "You're terrible at interviewing," blah, blah, blah....

That's called "a conversation not worth having." Whether those things are true or not, they don't empower you in any way. They just make you a little crazy. If you're alone—and when you're looking for work, you often are—that negative voice gets louder. Try to step back for a moment and realize that these conversations are merely *interpretations* born out of isolation. And if you can't step back, at least take some steps to muffle the negativity to manage your fear and anxiety. You may be bearing down too hard when what you need is to distract yourself. Give yourself permission to do that.

80.
Exercise

Exercising is good for you. It releases endorphins. If you exercise routinely while you're looking for work, it will also give your day some structure. Additional benefits include the following:

- You'll look better.

- Your mood will be enhanced.

- Your well-being will benefit.

- You'll feel a sense of accomplishment.

If you can't reach your goal of finding work during a given week, at least you reached your goal of, say, going to the gym four times and working out for 90 minutes each time. Yes, I know it's not the same as finding work. You'll need to play games with yourself—to fool yourself during your "looking for work" period into believing that you spent your time productively and accomplished *something*.

You may feel that whatever you do when you're not being paid to work is a waste of time, that your life is "on hold," or that you're somehow worthless if you're not a productive member of the labor force. But what you're *actually* doing—what you need to own and be fully present to with both your mind and body—is looking for work and supporting that effort in any positive way you can. Yes, going to the gym is a distraction. So what? That could be one of the things you need to do to keep yourself sane and support your well-being.

While you're searching for work, it's important that you find alternative ways of reminding yourself of your ability to accomplish things. It's good for your self-confidence. Exercise is a wonderful way to do this. Create a routine—say, 30 minutes on an elliptical machine, followed by a certain number of bench presses, curls, etc., and 20 minutes of stretching. Then increase your time on the elliptical, the number of reps in your weight training, and the amount of time you're stretching. Yes, I know it's not the same as finding a job, but you can't look for work 24/7. You might as well use the time you *can't* look for work to do something else productive.

81.

Compress Your Day

During the times in my life when I've had to look for work, one of the secrets I've learned is that there were only so many people to call, so many people available to meet, and so many postings I could answer. In other words, there was a finite number of things I could do in a day. If I felt I had done everything I could that day, then I considered it a productive one.

How many hours did it take to accomplish that finite number of things? Typically four, maybe five. And what did I do with the rest of the day? When I was younger, I sat around the house and worried. As I got older, I learned to compress my day. I realized that if I limited the amount of time I gave myself to accomplish something, I'd get it done—and most likely in a more efficient manner. So I'd allot four hours to a four-hour task. Then, being confident in my ability to get my work done, I'd spend the rest of the day doing something entirely different. I might even start the day by watching a movie, going to a museum, or hanging out at a coffee shop!

The work would be waiting for me when I got back—and when I did, I would have no time to waste, worry, or think. All I could do was get to work. As a result, I was more focused and worked with greater efficiency. I didn't pretend I needed eight hours to do what only required half as much time. By distracting myself, I kept out of my head and got the job done that needed to be done. I've always found this technique to be an excellent way to manage my day while keeping my spirits up.

82.

Lean on Your Friends

When you ask for support, you may be pleasantly surprised to find that you can get it. When I was single and unemployed, the toughest part of my day was right after I woke up. I felt disconnected from the world. So rather than feel sorry for myself, I called on my friends to get me through it. One friend volunteered to have me call her every morning at 8:00 a.m. We had our daily agenda: How was I feeling? What was I thinking about? What were my plans for the day? What did I propose to do in connection with finding work? What measurable results did I promise to produce? The next morning, during our 8:00 a.m. call, I reported my results.

These daily phone calls provided a number of benefits. For one, I felt connected. I was talking to someone other than myself. I also felt understood and supported. These calls were no pity party. My friend knew I had a goal in mind and specific tasks I needed to do every day to reach it. She was not interested in hearing me complain. She supported my better nature. While she was sympathetic, this was a *business* call.

These phone calls helped to ground me and to focus me on the job(s) at hand every day. I knew I had someone on my team who was confident I would find work (which I eventually did), who supported my efforts, and who kept me on target during the entire process. We talked for about 10 minutes every morning for about six or seven weeks (we took the weekends off). It obviously required a time commitment on her part, and she was happy to do it. The main thing was that she was there for me. That's what friends are for. You might want to find a committed listener of your own.

83.

Be Coachable

Years ago, the United Negro College Fund adopted its motto: "A mind is a terrible thing to waste." After being a career mentor and coach for many years, I've updated that motto to read as follows: "A *coach* is a terrible thing to waste." Whatever brilliant insights I have or spot-on advice I may offer, if my client or student is not receptive—if he doesn't listen and *apply* the coaching—then I might as well being talking to my cat.

The ability to listen without judgment is perhaps the most valuable communication tool we possess as human beings. This requires more than just politely waiting for the coach to finish talking until it's your turn to share your opinion. Being coached requires humility—the realization that in some cases, you may have no idea what you need to do. There will be times during your quest to find work when things will get tough. You'll feel like you've run out of ideas and options. When that happens, surrender to the coaching.

I teach a course called "Critical Thinking," but the practice of critical thinking itself also provides the foundation for many of my other, seemingly unrelated courses. I've reduced critical thinking to just two words: "How about?" In other words, you don't have all the answers. You don't or can't see all the possibilities. In the midst of a job or work search, when you've executed your battle plan every day and done everything you're supposed to but you're still not getting the results you're after, surrender.

Look to your friends. They're less involved than you and have a better perspective on the matter. They will be able to see openings that, in your frustration—maybe to the point of resignation or even terror— you can't see. Be smart and gracious enough to get out of the way. Shut up, listen, and follow their advice. "But," you protest, "I've done that already." Maybe you haven't. Or maybe it's time to do it again— or in a different way. Allow the people who love you to lighten your psychic load and offer you strategies and tactics you may never have thought of (despite your infinite wisdom). Listen…and lighten up. It's *just* looking for work. You're not in an ER, and no one's going to die.

84.

Flip Burgers

Be prepared for times when you feel you're going to go crazy if you don't find paid work. Some kind of work. *Anything.* You just need to get back into the game. I've been there, and it's okay to feel that way—and to act on it. You can get on Craigslist and find some sort of hourly part-time job. You need not consider it a comedown or a failure on your part, or that somehow you've given up.

So much of life is a matter of attitude—and attitude is often based on your interpretation of events. So let's create an empowering interpretation of why you're taking an hourly job doing something that's *way* below your capabilities: First of all, you're not giving up. You're maintaining your sanity. This job isn't forever. You just need a little structure for a short time. You need to earn some money for your labors, to contribute in some way to someone's organization, to feel part of a team.

This strategy you've *chosen* to pursue temporarily to keep sane and do *something* is known as "flippin' burgers." The term comes from the idea that when you're down on your luck and life seems hopeless, you are willing to do *whatever it takes* to get by. For me, that's sales. As someone once told me, "If you can sell, you'll never starve." It may not literally be flippin' burgers, but it's something.

Your version of "flippin' burgers" may be bussing tables or doing database entry in an office. Whatever it is, congratulations! You did what you had to do to get by financially and emotionally. This job won't last forever and you'll probably be able to quit in a short time. But you can feel good about yourself—which may be the whole point.

Besides, sometimes doing something very different can shake things up. I've found that going off track in this is often just the right move—suddenly, seemingly out of nowhere, I'm getting calls for jobs I applied to months before. This short-term "money job" can buy you some time so the universe can catch up to you. You've shown you really *will* do whatever it takes to get through. You're tougher than you may have thought. Now maybe you know that you can—and will—eventually succeed!

14

PREMIUM MARKETING STRATEGIES

Just go out there and have fun…If you're having fun, the money will come.

—Willie Mays, Major League Baseball Player (1931–)

We are in the midst of a seismic shift in the nature of the working world. This chapter contains advice on dealing with this new world of work, including some ideas and strategies you may not have considered before.

85.

Investigate Growth Industries

Yes, I know. Your industry is [fill in your field here]. That's where you've always worked. It's what you know, and you're determined to find more work in your field—no matter what!

Hold on a minute. What if your industry is dying? (Think newspapers.) In that case, you're going to have to shift gears. There may well be no more work for you (or anyone else) in your field if it's gone the way of the video-rental store. It's nothing personal—many other people who called your industry their home are no longer going to be able to do what they've been doing their whole lives. Things have just dried up. Why are you surprised? Did you not see this coming—or were you in denial?

In the 1990s, after they tore down the Berlin Wall and broke up the Soviet Union, the Cold War ended. That meant that all the weapons we were making to prepare ourselves for a possible showdown with the Communists were no longer needed. Massive layoffs in the aerospace industry ensued. Many engineers who went to work straight out of college for big companies with huge government contracts were, for the first time in their lives, forced to look for work. Some of them had never even written a résumé before! Imagine their shock and dislocation. This was the work they expected to be doing until they retired.

Don't be caught flatfooted when it's *your* turn. And trust me, it will be. This is going to happen to *every* industry at some point. Technology is simply moving too rapidly to spare anyone. No one is safe. You'll be constantly recareering—retraining and learning new skills that can move you over to other industries.

I, too, face this inevitability—and believe me, *I* don't like it either. Online education is replacing the classroom teacher and professor. Why? Simple. It's cheaper. ("Those bean counters ruin everything!") It's a fact: The nature of education will change. Will the quality suffer? Will students get shortchanged? In my opinion, yes and yes. But no one asked for my opinion. Change will happen to me—and you— no matter what we think or want.

We all need to be predictive and proactive. If you start with the presumption that your current field has a limited shelf life, you can immediately begin to research where the economy and our work culture are headed. Then you can plan and take specific steps to be ready *before* they downsize you. You can discover the future. What industries are coming up in the world? To use the newspaper industry as a model, people aren't reading newspapers as much as they used to—but they're still reading. *What* are they reading? Where are they doing their reading?

I'm inviting you to embrace change. The prospects are exciting. We will all be forced to create new ways to connect with the people we serve, to understand *their* needs and the best ways to reach them. We all have gifts to share and we'll be finding innovative ways to do just that. When you get to the other side of scary, the prospects are challenging and very exciting. I'm exploring distance learning. What are *you* going to be learning about in your field?

86.

Have a Project to Sell

When you're pursuing a new industry or repositioning yourself in an old one, here's a useful way to navigate uncharted waters. I'll use my friend Brent's experience as a blueprint. Brent lived in Washington, D.C., where he worked as a political consultant but wanted to move to Los Angeles. He had some experience in digital media and decided to leverage that while he looked for work in L.A.

What was innovative in his search was that he wasn't just selling *himself.* He also had a project to talk to people about. When we first met, I was a new technologies agent at the Agency for the Performing Arts. Brent and I were introduced through a mutual friend named Linda. The way she pitched him to me was that he was moving to the west coast and had a CD-ROM tour of the U.S. Capitol for which he was trying to get representation. The focus was on the project, not on Brent.

Brent and I met, and I was impressed—not so much with the project, which I didn't think had much commercial viability outside of Washington, but with the man himself. You could say the project was the loss leader so I'd buy the guy. I did. Brent and I are friends to this day, and because I liked him and was impressed with him, I helped him get connected while he was relocating. When I embrace a colleague, my policy, to paraphrase Ronald Reagan, is *"mi database es su database."* In other words, I was happy to introduce Brent to anyone I thought could help him feel more at home in Los Angeles.

Nowadays, Brent—always on the cutting edge of change—has been living and working in digital media for the past three years in Beijing, China. He's the poster child for both embracing change and going where the work is.

87.

Learn to Negotiate

As with public speaking, many people find negotiating to be intimidating. Really, though, it's not that difficult to become proficient in either skill. Two things will prepare you for negotiating:

- **Your sound bite**. As you've learned, your sound bite gives a clear sense of what you offer in the business world. It also gives you self-confidence because are able to articulate exactly what that offering is.

- **Your budget**. Your budget reveals in black and white the revenue you need to cover your nut.

Armed with this knowledge, you know where you stand and are ready to negotiate for work.

Whether you're discussing your salary at a new job, asking for a raise, or setting a price for a project with a client (or buying a car or a home—or anything else), you want to bear two numbers in mind: the amount you want and the amount you're willing to settle for. Let's use negotiating a salary as an example. Suppose you're going in for a second or third job interview and you know the subject of money will be addressed. The question is, what do you ask for? To answer this, you must do your homework—your due diligence about the company with which you're interviewing. Research the industry to learn what the pay range is for the job for which you're applying. Have some idea of how well they pay compared to their competitors. If you're going for a manager's job and the pay range is $48,000 to $55,000 annually, you want $55,000, of course. The question then becomes, how much do you *need*?

Unfortunately, there are no strict rules on how to navigate the negotiation process. Every situation is different, each with its own variables. Plus, you need to consider more than just salary. There are also benefits, vacation time, career opportunities, the length of your commute, the availability of flex time, and so on. Factoring in all of the above, you can pinpoint the amount you want—*and* the amount you can live with.

Here's one important rule of negotiating: Be prepared to leave with nothing. If you're living within your means, you should not be desperate when you walk in the room. In a negotiation, if you must close the deal—if you have to get something, no matter how insultingly low the offer—you've lost before you've even begun. You have no freedom to turn the deal down if it makes no sense. Go in with your budget in mind and don't take less than your lowest figure. You want the freedom to walk away from the table—perhaps disappointed, but with your dignity intact. Not every date ends in marriage, and not every negotiation results in a deal. Thank the people you met with, and move on.

But wait…you'd be surprised how often a failed negotiation plants the seeds for future deals. The people with whom you've been negotiating will leave the table with a clear sense of what you offer. They'll also know that you respect your own talents, that you are unwilling to shortchange yourself, and that you respect their needs and budget and are willing to find a middle ground. Finally, they've seen that you can accept that sometimes, despite both parties' best efforts, a meeting of the minds isn't possible. They've seen that you're willing to entertain alternatives, but smart and honest enough to recognize when something won't work. Those are all qualities that people value in the business world. Don't be surprised if your get a callback months later, either from the people with whom you negotiated, someone else inside the company, or even an outside associate of theirs. Even though the first negotiation didn't result in a deal, you left a positive impression. It's just like a sale. It wasn't a "no," it was a "not yet."

15

MORE ARTILLERY

In many situations that seemed desperate, the artillery has been a most vital factor.

General Douglas MacArthur, American General and
Field Marshal of the Philippine Army (1880–1964)

L ife is self-awareness and relationships. The former is how you're wired, and the latter how you're connected. All the effort you invest in establishing and growing your career is a matter of understanding and harnessing the first to improve the second. This chapter includes ideas and strategies to help you increase your effectiveness in connecting with your target audience.

88.
Arm Yourself

As always, the first place to look is at your audience. What do *they* need to see, hear, smell, taste, or touch to feel better about working with you? In your field, what convinces someone to hire you?

- If you're a graphic artist, it's samples of your work—both online and off.

- If you're a musician, it's inviting people (potential buyers) to hear your music and see you perform. That means inviting them to live shows and enabling them to easily download your music and watch your performances on YouTube.

- If you're a fashion designer, it's more than just sketches of your designs. Your audience wants to feel the fabric and see how the clothes drape on a model.

- If you're a chef, your audience wants to smell and taste your food. They don't simply want a description (the menu)—they want to *experience* it (the meal).

Develop relationships with colleagues and find mentors. These people will tell you what to prepare. Listen to them and follow their advice. Your colleagues and mentors can also advise you about what makes the sale. What represents you as a professional? Are your business cards appropriate for your field? Do they have all the information your audience will need to know what you do and how to find you? What other marketing documents (proposals, one-sheets, press kits, electronic press kits, websites, product samples, price sheets, etc.) do you need professionally prepared and ready to distribute?

I was recently given a presentation of a database program via tele-conference. As the buyer, I was the audience—*my* needs were the only ones that mattered. The company giving the presentation was not audience-centric, however. They weren't familiar with me. They hadn't done their homework. They displayed a list of the services they offered onscreen and then said that one of them was no longer available. That's sloppy work. They had quoted me a price a few weeks earlier, but during the call, they informed me that I should add a 20% contingency fee (which I might or might not have to dip into), and that the 20% could possibly increase. That's poor preparation. The entire experience was a textbook example of how to make a potential customer nervous about doing business with you. Don't approach *your* potential clients in this way. It's unprofessional. Be thoroughly prepared for every contingency. Make them *want* to do business with you.

89.
Get Your Ducks in a Row

As an employer, I have a right—indeed, a *responsibility*—to research everyone I might consider hiring for a job. I am looking for problems—the things that might eliminate the candidate. So you'd better believe I check each candidate's LinkedIn profile and Facebook page. I also search for them on Google, talk to their references, and talk to anyone in *my* network who may know—or knows someone who may know—the candidate. I'm looking to find the dirt, if there is any. This is standard operating procedure for *all* employers now. Your online presence and your reputation in your industry—that is, what people who know and have worked with you say about you—weigh very heavily in any employer's decision to hire you (or not).

On LinkedIn, I want to see that you're literate. (Presumably your résumé shows that you are, or you never would have gotten this far in the hiring process with me.) What have you chosen to highlight in your profile? A LinkedIn page is a business document. As such, it needs to be an impeccable representation of who you are.

Facebook is where the problems usually lie. For some reason, people think Facebook is the "anti-LinkedIn"—the place where they can let their hair down and have fun, like the bar they frequent at the end of the workweek. Well, guess what? I'm hiding in the "bar" and watching everything you do. Facebook is a public place. Don't you think I'd protect my own interests and see what you're doing there? You may have thought that photo you posted of you getting hammered with your college friends was cute and fun back then. Today, it's a turnoff to an employer. The same goes for any status updates you may have posted and comments you may have made.

Remember, in the working world, the employer almost always has the advantage. That is, there is often just one job, but many candidates. If you give me reason to believe that your past behaviors are not "past" and/or you were careless enough to post something potentially embarrassing, I will be moving on to another, less risky candidate. You—and everything that *ever* represents you—need to be thoroughly professional at all times. By the way, this includes your credit score and history. If you are having financial problems, I want no part of them. So clean them up and scrub your online presence *before* we meet. You're supposed to be offering me solutions to the problems I'm having, not giving me more problems to deal with!

90.
Network "Up"

I recently met with an alumnus who was originally from Korea. He was a U.S. citizen, but both his oral and written English skills were so poor that I knew we'd have a hard time placing him in a job. When I encouraged him to take an ESL course, he admitted that he knew his English was poor, but since all his friends were Korean, there was little to motivate him to improve his English.

Many people I work with get themselves mired in environments that undermine the progress they need to make to reach their goals. In the case of this alum, in addition to ESL work, he realized he needed to make friends with people who spoke English as their native language. This would force him to speak English, which would improve his language skills and increase his chances for finding a job in the U.S.

Others spend too much time with friends who are in the same predicament as they are. If you're a wannabe anything, don't hang out with other wannabes. The conversations will inevitably degenerate into pity parties, with everyone sharing "how tough it is out there." This serves no purpose other than to keep you stuck where you are in your career.

Instead, network "up." Make it your business to spend time around people who are at a more advanced level in your field. It ups your game. For example, if you play tennis with someone at your own level, you don't have much chance of improving. But if you play with *better* players, your game *has to* improve. Unless you're a professional tennis player, what you're doing—or not doing—in your career is far more important than tennis. You need to improve your chance of finding work, so you'll want to develop and nurture relationships with people who can pull you up and into *their* level—who are already where you want to be. These are the people you can learn from.

If you want to be skinny, hang around skinny people. If you want to be rich, hang with rich people. If you want to find work/move up in your field, spend time with the people who are already there.

91.

Target Companies

By now, no doubt you're voraciously reading everything you can get your eyeballs on about your industry of choice. And in doing so, you may have found that certain companies—their culture, their mission, their vision, their products and services, how they treat the people they work with—resonate for you. You can envision yourself working with them or for them.

This presents yet another route you can take to find work that is both creatively and financially satisfying. Dive in to your granular database and locate people who work for said company or know someone who does. In addition to reading *about* the company, try "reading" the people who have worked there. Begin modeling yourself after them. What type of person does this company like to hire? Do you fit that mold? If not, what do you need to do so that you are recognized as someone who belongs there?

As always, be open to coaching from people who have preceded you there. Follow their advice. Get the additional training they suggest, if that's what you need. That could be anything from learning Mandarin to getting another degree to changing your wardrobe. Begin spending time with the company's employees and consultants by joining industry associations to which they may belong. Go where they go—softball leagues, bars, charity events, etc. Learn if you really *would* be a fit to their culture, and be open to the possibility that the answer may be no. But if you *do* feel a kinship, make friends and have those friends "invite" you to join the company.

I'm hoping you'll apply all the resources in this book to your quest. But perhaps one of the most important tips you've discovered is how to use the people you know—and those you will meet and get to know—as resource centers. *Everyone* has ideas. Think of these people as walking books—or libraries—who need to be mined to open you to the ideas, options, and possibilities you hadn't thought of before.

92.
Revisit Your Strategy

If you're hitting a wall and nothing's working, it might be time to take another look at what you're doing and possibly adjust your strategy. This is where your friends and colleagues can prove invaluable. You may need to consider some drastic steps—things that, before, seemed inconceivable.

During my senior year in college, I lived in the San Francisco Bay Area. I decided that what I really wanted to do in my career was to work in television production. I began to network. Through a friend, I met with the program manager of a local television station. He told me that if I *really* wanted to work in TV production at the network level, I needed to move to Los Angeles.

To many people who live in the Bay Area, L.A. is like a combination of Sodom and Gomorrah—a cultural wasteland where everyone's superficial and phony. You simply *do not* move to L.A. Moving to L.A. means selling out and abandoning all your principles. I believed that, too.

But you go where the work is. If I wanted to work in television production, I had three choices:

- New York…but I was *from* there and had zero interest in moving back
- A small market…but I was a big-city boy, and living in a small town was not an option
- Los Angeles

How badly did I want the work? Was I willing to do whatever it took to pursue my dream? In a word, yes. I moved to Los Angeles. And yes, many of the things I was warned about turned out to be true. It can be superficial. The architecture is generally terrible. There is an enormous emphasis on appearance—and more plastic surgery than I've ever seen anywhere. But I built a career there in television production at the network level.

What are you willing to do to make *your* dreams come true?

93.
Consider Shifting to a New Field

What if you weren't supposed to win—or even *work*—in your field? Could you shift gears? There's a Garth Brooks song that goes, "Some of God's greatest gifts are unanswered prayers." I've heard this sentiment expressed as "Rejection is God's protection." It may be that the universe is sending you a message: that you're not built for the job you seek.

Could you consider abandoning the field you've dreamed of working in? Could you entertain such a seismic shift in your thinking—and actions? You'd be dealing with the difference between being committed to something and being *attached* to it. In the former case, you're willing to do whatever you have to do to succeed. In the latter instance, you've given yourself no alternative—you *have* to succeed. There is simply no alternative.

It's possible you'll discover that you really *do* want to continue in the field you've chosen. In that case, you'll need to recommit to it and create new strategies to reach your goal. But *maybe* it's time to take stock, realize you've done your best, and it just isn't working. Maybe you need to try something else—something new.

If so, don't disparage yourself or feel as if you're a failure. So much in life is how we frame or spin things. Rather than label yourself in a negative manner, how about creating and owning an interpretation that says, "I tried it, I gave the effort a sufficient amount of time to develop, but it didn't work. The most sober, intelligent, and business-like decision to make was to try something new." Businesses do this all the time—and *you're* a business too, right? As General Douglas MacArthur once put it, "We are not retreating, we're just advancing in a different direction."

16

BUILDING YOUR ONLINE FOOTPRINT

The key to great marketing is remembering that even though you're all about your brand, your customer is not. As with any first date, getting a second date depends on doing your best to learn more about what the other person is interested in, and directing the conversation in that direction.

—Gary Vaynerchuk, Social Media Strategist (1975–)

A *meme* is a style, behavior, symbol, practice, or idea that spreads—like a virus—from one person to another. Memes are sort of "cultural genes." They can both self-replicate and mutate. They can be transmitted via writing, speech, gestures, rituals…or online.

The explosion of online content—specifically, social media content that's mobile—is a culture-shifting trend, a meme of its own. This chapter looks at some of the leading social media platforms and how you can use them to connect to your audience, share with them, and ultimately find work.

94.

Do Business on LinkedIn

If you're looking for work, start with LinkedIn (www.linkedin.com), *the* leading online business community. You can't *not* be a part of it.

As with any social network, you can't just visit every so often. You need to fully participate. Saying "I have a LinkedIn page but I never use it" is like buying a ticket to a dance party and not dancing. Why bother? If you're going to derive the benefits, you need to actively engage. Consider this: LinkedIn now has more than 200 million members. Not only that, almost 3 million *companies* have their own LinkedIn page. LinkedIn is where you go to make connections and do deals.

Think of the time you spend on LinkedIn as an investment in your career. It will increase your hipness/cool factor. Plus, you'll begin to develop relationships with people and companies you didn't even know existed before.

Three years ago, I found a job posting on LinkedIn. I didn't get the job, but the contacts I made became colleagues, and remain so to this day. They asked me to present with them at a conference, where I met some book publishers, which eventually resulted in this book! It just goes to show you how networking—including on LinkedIn— can lead directly to opportunities!

95.

Turn Facebook into a Marketing Tool

Facebook is the 500 pound gorilla of social media. It boasts more than 1 billion active users (50% of which are mobile users). Moreover, 20% of all page views in the United States are on Facebook. Yes, Facebook is *that* ubiquitous. Facebook also has some of the most cutting-edge analytics available. If you're selling anything—think: you and the services you offer—Facebook can tell you how you're doing and what you might need to adjust to make your marketing campaign more effective.

I recommend that you use Facebook to connect with people—all over the world—to build and enlarge your network of contacts. Call it *indirect marketing*. You can never have too many friends. The more people you know—and the more people who know about *you*—the more possibilities you create for yourself. Use Facebook as a long-range strategy. The relationships you develop and nurture here will pay off for you for years to come, in ways you cannot imagine right now.

With Facebook, your friends can act as agents in locating business trends and opportunities for you. It allows you to engage with people based on shared interests. It's like a giant affinity group portal. If you're selling something—including your own brand—think of Facebook not as the place where you close sales, but where you *open* them.

As with all marketing efforts, your activity on Facebook should be audience-centric. Your focus needs to be on what *they* care about, and on what you can do for them. Sound familiar? How successful you are with this is measured in large part by "likes." These tell you how many people were in some way moved by the content you shared and how much of an impact you made. In addition, if people share something of yours, it means they like it. As an added bonus, response time is virtually instantaneous. As you engage with people on Facebook, you create a community. They start to feel you are "one of them."

Connecting on Facebook is good practice for when you have to find—and work with—employers, clients, and customers. As with any form of communication, less is more. Remember that Facebook users are on the go and multitasking. Don't waste their time. Have fun with them instead.

96.

Gather Followers on Twitter

At first glance, Twitter (www.twitter.com) can seem like a toy. After all, what of importance can you possibly say in 140 characters?

Let's reframe this conversation. Twitter has more than 500 million users. That means there's *something* going on with it. I think Twitter's like a giant cocktail party. What you do on Twitter is "work the room," just like you do at a cocktail party. You connect and engage with the people you meet so they remember you. Of course Twitter's room is *much* bigger. In fact it's as big as…the world!

Twitter is about sharing news and information and building friendships. When you tweet, you can attach music, still photos, and videos. This enables you to "rebroadcast" interesting things you've seen or heard—to everyone! If you've ever gone to a cocktail party (or mixer or networking event) and pulled out your phone to share pictures of your kids (or dog or hamster), you get the idea. It's just that on Twitter, you share interests and make friends *everywhere*. (Can you see the opportunities?)

The people who use Twitter skew young, hip, and urban. It's a good place to track what's on trend. (You *are* looking at industries and companies that are forward-thinking, yes? Just checking.)

97.

Use Pinterest, Instagram, and Tumblr

It's important that you be aware of the latest trends in our culture. Given that so much of our culture is driven by what's happening online, that means you need to be aware of what people are doing there. Where there are people, there is commerce, and where there is commerce, there is work for you.

Here are three of the coolest and most popular social media platforms. I've hopefully included enough information about each of them to entice you into further exploration. As each of these is an *experience,* the most I can do is, like a good waiter, to describe what's on the menu. You're going to have to order the meal yourself!

Note that your goals in researching and engaging with these three sites are twofold. First, you want to get comfortable using new social media platforms. Second, you want to connect with people and form friendships. This is a long-term play. It's strategic, not tactical. You will need both strategy and tactics in your lifelong effort to market and promote yourself!

- **Pinterest (www.pinterest.com).** Boasting almost 50 million users, about 60% of whom are female (half of those being mothers), Pinterest is a visual discovery tool. People use it to collect ideas for various projects, interests, and hobbies; to plan trips and projects; to organize events; to save articles and recipes; and more. It's like online scrapbooking—but so much more. People use Pinterest to identify and share what they love and what inspires them—things that represent who they are and who they aspire to be.

- **Instagram (www.instagram.com).** This online photo-sharing, video-sharing, and social-networking service enables its users to take pictures and videos (of up to 15 seconds), apply digital filters to them, and share them. In addition to sharing these items on Instagram itself, users can also post them on a variety of other social-networking platforms, including Facebook, Twitter, Tumblr, and Flickr. Its 130 million active users upload some 40 million photos every day, which in turn generate a thousand comments *every second*! The content on Instagram skews artsy, so it provides an opportunity for users to show how creative they can be.

- **Tumblr (www.tumblr.com).** Tumblr is a two-fer—both a microblogging platform and a social networking site. This community of cool lets users post multimedia and other content to a short-form blog, which other users can follow. Tumblr hosts more than 174 million blogs, has 132 million monthly unique users, and boasts 60 million new posts every day! Interestingly, it's the #1 ranked site for average minutes spent per visit (Facebook is #3). Tumblr's demographic is largely the 18–34 year old market so coveted by television networks. That group doesn't watch much television any-more, however—partly because they're on Tumblr! Think of Tumblr as an art gallery or exhibition space largely for musicians, photographers, and graphic artists, who are given artistic control of their work. The look is less text and more visual. It's eye candy, full of animated GIFs, often used as an art form. Tumblr is art on your phone. It's like watching a never-ending movie of beautiful images.

98.

Create a Fan Base via WordPress, Yahoo! Groups, and Google+

We turn now from "cool" to "cool and somewhat more useful for doing business." These are three sites you should know about and use:

- **WordPress (www.wordpress.com)**. This free blogging tool and content management system is used by almost 20% of the top 10 million websites. With more than 60 million sites in all, it's the most popular blogging system around. This is where you may want to have your blog reside (we've agreed you're going to be blogging so you can establish your credibility as an authority in your field, right? Just checking).

- **Yahoo! Groups (groups.yahoo.com)**. This is one of the world's largest collections of online discussion boards. You can think of each board as sort of a cross between an electronic mailing list and an Internet forum. You can read and post group messages on a group's page via email. Members of the group can decide whether to receive individual messages, daily digests, or special delivery emails informing them of events, relevant articles, topics for discussion, etc. Or, they can just opt to read posts on the site. Groups can be public or members-only. I belong to a *lot* of groups, both on Yahoo! and LinkedIn. These include my high school graduating class, my college alumni association, my college fraternity, my graduate school alumni association, my doctoral program alumni association, and more. I also belong to several groups related to my industry, including groups for higher education, for-profit higher education, colleges and careers, career counselors, etc. I need to know what's going on in my field at all times. The same goes for you.

- **Google+ (plus.google.com)**. This is the second-largest social networking site in the world, after Facebook. It has 540 million monthly active users, who also use it to interact with Gmail.

All of these—and other sites you'll discover on your own—present an opportunity for you to learn, to connect with your colleagues worldwide, and to have them get to know you.

99.

Use These Sites to Find Work

Following are some wonderful online resources that you can use to help you find work. These will complement your offline, face-to-face initiatives for building your network.

- **Indeed (www.indeed.com).** This metasearch engine for job listings is currently available in 53 countries and 26 languages. It is the most visited job site in the United States, reaching more than 100 million unique visitors each month. The site, which is searchable and offers job alerts, aggregates job listings from thousands of websites, including job boards, newspapers, associations, and company career pages. For my students, who typically seek low-level or entry-level jobs, it's the first site they visit. It's very handy and easy to use.

- **Freelancer (www.freelancer.com) and Elance (www.elance.com).** These are just two of many online marketplaces for freelance talent to connect with people who are hiring. If you do freelance work, these sites are certainly worth a shot. Because we live in a global economy and so much of our work is now done virtually, your potential market is worldwide!

- **Alexa (www.alexa.com).** With a degree in Sociology and another one in Broadcast Communication Arts, I am—and always will be—a student of media. Not surprisingly, Alexa is one of my favorite websites. The site, which is visited by more than 8.5 million people each month, collects data on browsing behavior (read: online cultural trends). This data then forms the basis for the site's Web traffic reporting. Alexa provides this traffic reporting—as well as global rankings and other information—for about 30 million websites. So how can Alexa help you? It provides an accurate early warning system for the future of the online world. Alexa can alert you to what's new, what people are doing, and where you need to be.

100.

Use These Sites for Sales and Marketing Research

Sales and marketing. What's the difference? Marketing is the research, the preparation, the soft sell, the strategy, the artillery. Sales is the boots-on-the ground, face-to-face, close the deal, tactical part—the infantry. I've done both sales and marketing. You'll need to do both, too. Following are a few sites I've found to be excellent resources for sales and marketing:

- **EventsEye (www.eventseye.com).** This free website lists trade shows, exhibitions, conferences, and business events all over the world. You'll need to know about events in *your* field, right? Because you'll be attending them to make contacts, market yourself, sell your wares, and find work, right? Just checking.

- **Acronym Finder (www.acronymfinder.com).** As a culture, we are acronym-crazy. Every industry, including mine, has its own set of acronyms, like a secret code or a secret handshake, with new ones created all the time. Acronym Finder is my secret weapon. This searchable database of more than 4 million acronyms makes me feel that I'm as hip and up to date as everyone else in my field—which is important when I'm trying to market myself or make a sale. Checking this site should be SOP for you from now on.

- **ConstantContact (www.constantcontact.com).** This online marketing company offers tools for email marketing, social-media marketing, online surveys, event marketing, digital storefronts, and local deals, primarily to small businesses, nonprofit organizations, and membership associations. It boasts more than 500,000 customers. SurveyMonkey (www.surveymonkey.com) is similar, and also very useful.

- **StumbleUpon (www.stumbleupon.com).** This discovery engine finds and recommends Web content to users. Its features enable users to discover and rate Web pages, photos, and videos that are personalized to their tastes and interests using the principles of peer sourcing and social networking.

101.

Beware the Downside of Electronic Media

Be sure you use all the aforementioned social media platforms inter-actively (push an Instagram picture on Twitter, etc.). In other words, cross-pollinate. All social media platforms have a distinct culture. Be aware of each one and how best to use them. Always respect the platform!

Staying ahead of the curve should be your standard operating pro-cedure from now on. Remember: Mobile is your friend, social media is your friend, technology is your friend. If you feel "friend" is too strong a word, substitute "tool."

All that being said, I'm going to end things on a cautionary note. Technology is great, but nothing will ever replace face-to-face com-munication. You cannot replicate being in the same room, sharing ideas with others. Great communication skills—the ability to hear and lead people—are prized in the workplace. People who make the big bucks are the ones who can relate to and empower those around them. If you can do that, people will want to work with you. Your facility and proficiency with technology are a wonderful asset, but it's the relationships you build that will *really* make a difference.

Hang out, make friends, find work.